Superlatives U S A

Capital Travels Books

Other titles in the series include the following:

Barging in Burgundy: Boating, Exploring, Wining & Dining by Erasmus Kloman

How to Stay in London for Less: Short-term Apartments Ideal for All Travelers by Diana and Ronald Jensen

Steeles on Wheels: A Year on the Road in an RV by Donia and Mark Steele

Washington, DC from A to Z: The Look-Up Source for Everything to See & Do in the Nation's Capital by Paul Wasserman and Don Hausrath

Superlatives USA

The Largest, Smallest, Longest, Shortest, and Wackiest Sites in America

MELISSA L. JONES

CAPITAL TRAVELS

Capital Books, Inc.
P.O. Box 605
Herndon, Virginia 20172-0605
www.capital-books.com

ISBN 1-931868-85-9 (alk.paper)

Text Design by Susan Mark

Library of Congress Cataloging-in-Publication Data

Jones, Melissa L. (Melissa Louise), 1972–
Superlatives USA : the largest, smallest, longest, shortest, and wackiest sites in America / Melissa L. Jones.—1st ed.
p. cm.
Includes index.
ISBN 1-931868-85-9 (alk. paper)
1. Historic sites—United States—Guidebooks. 2. Curiosities and wonders—United States—Guidebooks. 3. United States—Guidebooks. I. Title.
E159.J66 2005
973—dc22 20040183

Printed in the United States of America on acid-free paper that meets the American National Standards Institute Z39-48 Standard.

First Edition

10 9 8 7 6 5 4 3 2 1

This book is dedicated to
the coolest, kindest husband—Matt Kish,
and the many other friends and family members
who've shared a sandwich at 70 miles per hour.

CONTENTS

ACKNOWLEDGMENTS

From Maine to Arizona to Georgia to Washington State, I owe huge thanks to all the people that helped with this book. There is a piece of every state in here. From the people at Capital Books in Virginia who wanted to publish it to the lady in southern Arizona who told me the story behind the world's biggest rose bush, at least one person in every state helped in some way and they won't all be named here. They included staff at the tiniest chambers of commerce, preservationists in North Carolina, gift shop workers, restaurant staff in California, and the insanely efficient public relations people in New York. Countless people gave directions, explained the earth's crust, interpreted history, and told me how to find an open auto store when my windshield wiper flew off on the freeway outside Baltimore on July 4. They work at universities, the National Park Service, state parks departments, and small mom-and-pop operations. Thanks!

Thanks to Matt who provided encouragement, computer hardware, back rubs, and did more than his share of chores during this process. Thanks to my parents for instilling in me a love for travel. Thanks to my many friends who have helped me know the joy of a good trip while sleeping in cars, waking up with food in my mouth, and eating outdoors.

Thanks to Megan Johnson, Christy Karl and my former coworkers in Oregon and Arizona, and friends all over who encouraged me to follow my bliss. Thanks to my mom for not making me call everyday when I was driving across country by myself. Thanks to my gracious friends and family who killed me with kindness when they barbecued steaks on their patios, made homemade pancakes before heading to work in Minneapolis, burned copies of their CDs, bought me dinners in Phoenix and rural Wisconsin, offered to buy me a car battery in Columbus, suggested the hot tub in San Diego, shared their houses with me in Chicago, Boston, and New York. Thanks to the friends who took time off work to play Frisbee and who didn't mind driving the long way to the world's largest six pack. Thanks to Laurie Notaro and Zoe Trope and the people in my McMenamins writing group for writing and inspiring others to do the same. Thanks to Noemi Arthur for wanting to publish this book and everyone at Capital Books who worked to get it together. Thanks to my 1995 Mazda Protégé for taking me back and forth across the States and Canada with nary a problem over 185,000 miles. (And Mazda didn't pay me to write that, even though I made a brief attempt to get a free car from them for my last trip.) And of course, thanks to all the giant paint ball makers in the world who give the rest of us something cool to look for on the horizon.

INTRODUCTION

You probably haven't had to consider superlatives since your last fifth grade English assignment. In simple terms, a superlative is the most something—the biggest, cheesiest, craziest, whatever "est" you want.

This is a collection of American superlatives you can visit, with a few twists. This is not the *Guinness Book of Records*. We do not have strict guidelines for the classification of a "superlative." You didn't have to make an edible, regulation donut to get in this book. Your giant fire hydrant doesn't have to be fully operational. We're generally just looking for a good photo or a good story. Fake stuff is a superlative in our book as much as real stuff.

Some superlatives are the biggest, smallest, tallest things not just in the United States, but in the world. Other superlatives have brethren. There are a few big eggs out there, several large rocking chairs, and a surprising number of giant frying pans. They are not all in here, not because they're not worthy, but because we tried not to duplicate too many things.

You will find regional traits among some entries. A lot of old stuff happened on the East Coast when the pilgrims started building bars and court houses. On the West Coast, we have a lot of interesting geological features. In the Midwest and South, you'll find many superlatives tied to the local agriculture. Some states have a lot more superlatives than others. That doesn't mean we don't like some states more than others. It just means that some states are bigger than others and some of the superlatives were easier for us to find, or we lived in that state and knew about it. We found a lot more biggest than littlest, and we think that's because this is America, and as a culture we seem to appreciate big things more than small things. Also because it's easier to see giant things from a moving car.

This book not comprehensive. Every year a new superlative is created. Others are not all accessible. For example, there is a woman in Las Vegas who has a giant collection of refrigerator magnets, which we'd love to see, but she doesn't necessarily want a bunch of salty people coming over to see them. She told us that some of them are in the Guinness museum in Las Vegas.

There is also a guy who has a collection of hair from famous people. My point is that every cool thing out there is not in here. But we'd like to learn about other superlatives, so please send me information on good stops at melissa@superlativesusa.com. Some of these sites are as grassroots as they come. They are in a person's front yard, fully supported by one or two people. If you are driving a long distance to reach one, consider calling ahead or doing some more research to be sure it hasn't been relocated by a recent tornado or shut down due to lack of funding.

The beauty of putting together this book was reveling in the great diversity of the United States. A lot of cool stuff happens in the U.S., from the tallest trees in California to the smallest post office in Florida. Yes, we have great sports teams and gigantic companies that make a ton of money, but we're not talking about that. We're talking about Amish people driving a buggy down a Wisconsin highway—a tradition maintained despite the road race going on around them, the South Dakota artist who turned a farm into a sculpture garden, and the joy of passing through the Indiana town with a radio station that plays a song you haven't heard 20 times in the past week. We're also talking about cheeseburgers at 9:30 a.m., cities where the streets are named after someone Polish, in cities where the street names are in Spanish in states named after Native American tribes.

We included directions as clearly as possible, but people will be coming from different directions, and we're not perfect. There were many times when we had no idea where our superlative was when we arrived in the town where it is located. If you get lost, stop and ask someone for directions. Half the fun of these sites is talking to the people who live around them. We got tons of help finding these things from the lady at the Kokomo pharmacy, the Birnamwood gas station attendant, the random Redwoods camp host, and others. Don't be shy; people want to help, and it's always fun watching people react to questions like, "Do you know where the talking cow is?"

When visiting, we recommend taking a photo of yourself in front of the superlative. If nothing else, this helps you get out of the car. We know what it's like when you are already running late. But in the long run, will an extra 10 minutes really matter when you can have a photo of yourself in a drive-through tree? That's one for the grandkids.

Having a buddy, spouse, or relative along for the ride usually makes stopping more appealing, because you can blame him when you're late or get lost. And he can talk you into ice cream or hot chocolate.

If you are traveling alone, which I have done many times, just bring a camera with a timer. You'd be amazed at the great angles you can get when you are forced to set your camera up on the hood of your car, hanging from the branch of a tree, or on the rail of the largest porch swing.

ALABAMA

Largest Office Chair
Anniston, AL

Our vast country contains many chairs: rocking chairs, mahogany chairs, Adirondack chairs. Many of them are giants. We do not have them all here, just enough to handle Goldilocks and maybe a bear. This one in Alabama is so big, you can park a semi under it! "We have people from all over the country come and stand across the street and make pictures of it," said Richard Ammons, the warehouse manager at Miller's Office Furniture and Steel. The chair was built in 1981 and is particularly appealing because it reminds us that we're not in a cubicle, at least for today. It's made of steel and is 31 feet tall.

➨ **Directions:** Head north on U.S. Highway 431 toward Anniston, seven miles north of Interstate 20. Take Highway 202 west for two blocks. Go left on Noble Street. The chair is located at 625 Noble Street at Miller's Office Furniture and Steel.

Largest Collection of Giant Peanuts
Dothan, AL

You might have heard about the artistic cow movement that swept through the country, which provided artistically decorated fake cows in cities across the land. But what about dozens of five foot peanuts in a town of 58,000 people? Dothan's peanuts are decorated and placed around town. There's an Elvis peanut, a flying superhero peanut, a cheerleader peanut, a hybrid potato/peanut Mr. Peanut Head, a paper boy peanut, and many others that don't even look like peanuts. They wear hats. They have wings. They carry baseball bats. The Dothan Downtown Group started the project to help fund murals in town. Since the project began, more than 40 peanuts have gone up. Anyone can buy a peanut, but there are certain rules about what you can do with them.

"You can't have anything ugly," said Susan Tatom, who works for the local chamber of commerce.

➨ **Directions:** Dothan is located in the southeast corner of Alabama, accessible from several highways. The peanuts are spread around town. For more information, visit www.dothanalcvb.com/peanuts.htm or call the Downtown Group at 334-793-3097.

Largest Cast Iron Statue
Birmingham, AL

Vulcan was the Roman god of fire and the patron of metal workers. This version is godlike for sure—55 feet tall. The statue was created for the St. Louis World's Fair in 1904. Alabama civic leaders wanted a monument to the state's mineral and manufacturing resources. Vulcan was made in a Birmingham foundry by local men using Birmingham iron mined on Red Mountain. Men worked 60 hour weeks to get the statue finished in four months. He is the largest cast iron statue in the world and the largest statue ever made in the United States.

Credit: Vulcan Park

Upon Vulcan's arrival at the fair in St. Louis, city officials from San Francisco and St. Louis offered to buy the statue but Birmingham leaders wouldn't sell it. However, getting him back home after the fair wasn't easy. He lost his spear somewhere on the railroad between St. Louis and Birmingham and was kicked off the train and dumped beside the tracks due to unpaid freight bills. By 1939, he'd finally found a home on a 123-foot pedestal looking over the city. In 1946, he became an activist and got a neon torch that would glow red for 24 hours after any traffic accident, reminding the city of highway safety. In 1971, he got a new pedestal and platform and gift shop. In 1999, he had to come down for first aid for his cracks and corrosion. He was back in business in March 2004.

➡ **Directions:** Vulcan is located at 10-acre Vulcan Park, 1701 Valley View Drive. From Interstate 65, take the Oxmoor exit and turn right on Oxmoor. Go right on Valley Avenue. The entrance is 1.5 miles ahead.

The tower is open from 10 A.M. to 10 P.M. Monday through Saturday. Sunday hours are 1 P.M. to 10 P.M. Admission is $6 for adults and $5 for children ages 5 to 12. For more information, visit www.vulcanpark .org or call 205-933-1409.

ALASKA

Fastest Glacier
Near Valdez, AK

Columbia Glacier, in Prince William Sound, is the fastest moving glacier in the world. It is more than 430 square miles and it moves 40 yards a day. Since 1982, Columbia Glacier has shrunk by seven miles, calving (or splitting off) chunks of ice into the sea of Prince William Sound, near Valdez. Tidewater glaciers like this one are generally visited by boat.

According to the folks at the U.S. Geological Survey, glaciers form when more snow falls than melts over a period of years, and the snow is compacted into ice and becomes thick enough to move. The Alaska Almanac estimates there are 100,000 glaciers in the state.

➤ **Directions:** Columbia Glacier is 30 miles from Valdez.

Tallest Mountain
Mount Denali/McKinley, AK

The 20,320 foot peak in Alaska is the tallest mountain in North America. Denali is the name the Athabascan tribe gave the peak in the Alaska Range. Denali means "high one." White folks started calling it McKinley after former senator and president William McKinley. In 1980, the name Mt. McKinley National Park was officially changed to Denali National Park and Reserve. The state of Alaska has officially changed the name back to Denali, but not everyone else (like the National Park Service) has. The debate over the name on the peak continues.

The park gets more than 300,000 visitors annually. Few climb to the peak, but when they do, it's typically between May and July. Each season, roughly 1,000 climbers attempt the peak. The later summer months are warmer, but melting snow makes crossing glaciers more dangerous. Even then, weather conditions are extreme. The mountain, which is very close to the Arctic Circle, gets storms from the Gulf of Alaska and the Bering

Sea. The cold and altitude is debilitating and the terrain treacherous. Temperatures can range from 90 degrees Fahrenheit to 50 degrees below zero. Climbers must carry off everything that they bring on the mountain, including their own waste.

It's much easier to look at the peak, but you need a clear day for that. The park has three visitor centers to help you find your way and plan activities. Each has different hours so check ahead of time.

➤ **Directions:** For more information, contact the National Park Service at www.nps.gov/dena/ or at 907-683-2294.

Largest National Forest
Tongass National Forest, Southeast Alaska

Bears, eagles, salmon, mountain goats . . . all this and more is captured in the Tongass National Forest, which covers a thick part of Southeast Alaska. The forest covers 17 million acres stretching from Juneau to Sitka, and Ketchikan, and beyond. There are cabins, dog sledding, an ocean, and mountains to keep you busy. Not to mention the islands and trees. The Forest Service folks can help you with bear watching and glacier visits, as well as cabin rentals.

➤ **Directions:** The forest service has two visitor centers to help with information on Southeast Alaska. The Southeast Alaska Discovery Center is in Ketchikan and Juneau has the Mendenhall Glacier Visitor Center. For more information visit, www.fs.fed.us/r10/tongass/ or call 907-225-3101.

ARIZONA

Tallest Fountain
Fountain Hills, AZ

I hold a certain affinity for this disco looking fountain, because I used to watch fireworks from this park in my younger days. Today, the water is an unfamiliar blue-green color, but the water still shoots straight up into the sky (like a waterfall in reverse) before cascading into the giant lake below. Like many of the manmade lakes around Phoenix, you don't swim in it; you just look at it.

If the wind is right and you are in the right place, you can feel a mist from the fountain.

Author photo

A disc golf course, where you can toss a Frisbee-style disc into metal baskets spread around the park, surrounds the water; and after a long day of driving, the park also offers a nice place to find a tree and enjoy an ice cream cone.

Note that the park is irrigated with reclaimed wastewater and sometimes it smells like it. The fountain is not always on. It operates for 15 minutes on the hour from 9 A.M. to 9 P.M., but it was on for closer to 10 minutes last time we were here. The spout will automatically shut down if the winds are stronger than 10 miles per hour. On St. Patrick's Day, the water is dyed green.

The fountain was built in 1970 by a developer trying to lure people to Fountain Hills. Since then, Phoenix and the Valley of the Sun have exploded with growth. A newer fountain in St. Louis, Missouri is reported to be taller, but it only operates during the summertime.

➤ **Directions:** From Shea Boulevard turn north on Saguaro Boulevard and travel two miles to the park, on the right side of the street. For parking access, turn right on El Lago Boulevard (Lake in Spanish) where there are restrooms. Or for a better view with the mountains in the background, turn right on Panorama Drive. Parking lines the perimeter of the park. For more information, visit www.ci.fountain-hills.az.us/ or call 480-816-5152.

Biggest Sundial
Carefree, AZ

Ah, the sun! It seems hard to escape it at times in the Phoenix metropolitan area. In Carefree, on the northern outskirts of town, people wanted to show their respect to the great fireball in the sky in two ways: with time and with solar energy.

Author photo

John Yellot was inspired by a sundial he saw in India. In Jaipur, he saw a brick sundial that was 100 feet high with a gnomon—the part that casts the shadow—150 feet long. He brought the idea back to Arizona, where he modified the sundial to be a solar collector.

The upper surface has copper tubing containing water that absorbs some of the sun's radiant energy. The heated water is pumped into a Carefree office building.

Some believe it might have been the first solar collector in the state. The gnomon in Carefree is 62 feet long and points directly at the North Star. The tip is 35 feet above the surface of the solar plaza. The sundial still tells the time, but as one observer stated, most of us just wear watches now.

According to Carefree historians, local solar time is 27 minutes later than Mountain Standard Time, so the hour markers were adjusted accordingly.

The sundial was cared for by the local Kiwanis club until the town took it over in 1988. The sunburst, hanging from the gnomon, is seven feet in diameter. The sun illuminates it by day and at night, it has lights. A postcard from the area long ago shows the sundial in the middle of an empty desert.

➤ **Directions:** In the northern reaches of Scottsdale, Scottsdale Road turns into Tom Darlington Drive. If you're heading north on Tom Darlington, turn right, or east, on Wampum Way. (Watch for sundial signs.) From Wampum, you'll see the Town Hall and Post Office almost as soon as you make the turn; the sundial is behind them. Take left on Easy Street, which forms a loop around the Town Hall. For more information, visit www.carefree.org or call 480-488-3686.

Sunniest Spot
Yuma, AZ

Located right on the Arizona/California border, Yuma is a place most folks simply zoom past on their way between Phoenix and San Diego. But 160,000 residents call the place home, many of them seeking the warmth of the sun. Summer temperatures hit more than 100 degrees regularly, and nearby fields soak in the sun. With the help of water from the Colorado River, the area produces millions of dollars worth of lettuce, grain, hay, and cotton. The Colorado River flows through the town and residents can take a cool dip by visiting parks that offer beach access to the river. It's sunny in Yuma more than 90 percent of the daylight hours.

➤ **Directions:** Yuma is in between Phoenix and San Diego, on Interstate 8 on the Arizona/California border.

Largest Meteor Impact Crater
Meteor Crater, AZ

This is the largest impact crater discovered in the United States. The impact is estimated to have occurred 50,000 years ago, resulting in a crater nearly a mile wide and 500 feet deep.

Erosion has eaten away and leveled many of the craters on earth. Bigger impact sites do exist on earth but Meteor Crater remains one of the best preserved.

Meteor Crater is privately owned. In 1902, Daniel Barringer came to the meteor to see if he could mine iron from it. He thought the meteor would be buried under the floor of the crater, but in fact it had disintegrated.

➤ **Directions:** Meteor Crater is located between Flagstaff and Winslow, off I-40 at exit 233. Hours are 7 A.M. to 7 P.M. seven days a week. Admission is $12 for adults and cheaper for children and seniors. For more information, visit www.meteorcrater.com or call 800-289-5898.

Author photo

Smallest Museum
Superior, AZ

With a mere 154 square feet in this museum, you don't have to worry about getting lost between the ancient Egyptian artifacts and the Baroque paintings. One of the centerpiece exhibits at the World's Smallest Museum (that's its official name) is the Apache Tear Good Luck Stone, a type of obsidian found near Superior. The legend of the stone, as told by the Museum, dates back to the 1870s. Apaches were surrounded by U.S. Calvary at the top of Apache Leap Mountain. The Apaches chose to ride their horses off of Apache Leap rather than be taken prisoner by the enemy. When the wives and family of the men learned the news of the tragedy, they wept tears that turned to gemstones when they hit the ground. Other displays contain artifacts and stories from the Old West.

➨ **Directions:** The museum is located at 1111 W. U.S. Highway 60 in Superior, in between Phoenix and Globe. Admission is free. The museum is open every day, from 8 A.M. to 2 P.M., except Tuesdays and major holidays. Unlike most other superlatives in this book, this museum may have reduced hours in the summer because it's very hot in the central Arizona desert. Call ahead. For more information, visit www.worldssmallestmuseum.com or call 520-689-5857.

Biggest Canyon
Grand Canyon, AZ

If you haven't seen the Grand Canyon, it's time to start planning your trip. Words really can't describe the grandeur of the place . . . the terraced hills, the pinks, browns, and reds of the canyon. It is a remarkable sight to look out over the layers of the earth that took billions of years to develop.

The Colorado River and the earth's evolution have formed this place—a giant canyon that goes on and on for as far as the eye can see. The park covers more than 1.2 million acres on the Colorado Plateau.

The canyon is 277 miles long and its width ranges from seven to 42 miles across. It is 6,000 feet deep at its deepest point. The walls of the canyon show a geological record with some 40 identified layers that are still being studied today; the walls rise up a mile high and display a cross-section of earth that, in some places, is two billion years old. Inside the canyon you can see evidence of the Native Americans who lived there as well as the places where Powell's men explored by boat. The canyon is inhabited by California Condors, bats, lizards, snakes, turtles, endangered cactus species, bald eagles, spotted owls, bighorn sheep, and countless other creatures. Temperatures vary widely between the rims and the canyon floor, so bring clothing appropriate for both hot days and cool nights. In the winter, expect snow on the rims. The canyon is loaded with trails and opportunities for exploration.

➨ **Directions:** For more information, visit www.nps.gov/grca or call 928-638-7888.

Biggest Kachina
Tonto Hills, AZ

This 40-foot tall Kachina is the corn Kachina. Genuine Kachina dolls are made of the root of the cottonwood tree by Hopi and Zuni tribes. Kachinas are typically doll-sized and are carved to represent plants, animals, the sun, and the natural world. The dolls are used ceremonially in tribal dances and given to children as effigies of the spirits.

Nine cement sections were stacked on top of one another to make the Kachina this tall. Like its neighbor the sundial, the Kachina was constructed to entice homeowners to the area.

➨ **Directions:** Head north on Scottsdale Road until it turns into Tom Darlington. Go right on Cave Creek Road. Follow the road up until you see the Kachina.

Largest Rose Bush
Tombstone, Arizona

The largest rose bush, called Lady Banksia, covers 8,000 square feet and is nine feet tall. It is more than 100 years old and she just keeps getting bigger and better. The Lady Banksia has been called the biggest rose bush in the world. Her trunk circumference is more than 13 feet around. The folks at the inn say the bush was originally sent here from Scotland. A homesick young bride, who was staying at the boarding house, received some presents from her parents that included the rose bush.

➨ **Directions:** The rosebush is located at Rose Tree Museum and Books, 116 S. Fourth Street. From U.S. 80, turn south on Third Street and turn left on Toughnut Street. The museum is on the corner of Fourth and Toughnut. The museum is open everyday from 9 A.M. to 5 P.M. except Thanksgiving and Dec. 25. Admission is $3 for everyone 15 and older. For more information, visit www.tombstone.org or call 520-457-3326.

ARKANSAS

Biggest Spinach Can
Alma, AR

Okay, it's a water tower, but we really like giant things linked to local agriculture, primarily because it reminds us to eat more vegetables. Alma calls itself the spinach capital of the world, and this can attests to it. It's even got Popeye on it, the king spinach eater, who graces the cans of Allen Canning Company spinach products.

➨ **Directions:** The can be seen from the intersection of Highways 71 and 64.

Biggest Razorback Hog
Berryville, AR

Arkansas is Razorback country. And outside of Berryville, grazing in the Arkansas countryside is a Razorback hog kindly known as "the razorback hog."

Joe and Savannah Parkhill built the beast in 1976 and he has been carefully maintained since. He is a well-traveled hog, having gone to Washington D.C. for an appearance in the Cherry Blossom Festival. These days he's a regular in the local parades. He sits outside a store called Country Bazaar, where you can buy honey.

➨ **Directions:** The hog is located in front of the Country Bazaar store at 1241 Highway 62. He's about two miles west of Berryville.

Largest Watermelon
Bald Knob, AR

Every year, this giant watermelon takes a spin through the Bald Knob parade. On non-parade days, this watermelon rests at Ronnie's Produce Market. The melon is 25 feet long.

➨ **Directions:** The watermelon is located on Highway 167, just outside of Bald Knob on the north side of the city.

CALIFORNIA

Tallest Living Tree
Humboldt Redwoods State Park, CA

There is a catch here, because the people who run the park won't exactly tell you which tree is the tallest. They don't want people to hover around it, stomp the ground around the tree compacting the soil, or carve initials in bark that's older than texts about messiahs.

The parks folks will say, however, that eight of the tallest living trees in the world live within the park, and there are quite a few giants that are easy to see. The park is huge, with several exits off Highway 101, so it's not a bad idea to stop at the visitor's center for a map if you plan to explore quite a bit. The park is 52,000 acres, with 17,000 of them containing old growth redwoods.

We visited the towering figures in the Rockefeller Forest near the Alder Creek Campground, off Mattole Road. The Big Trees Area Loop Trail is five miles west of the Avenue of the Giants on Mattole Road, nine miles from the Visitor's Center. After crossing a creek in the big tree area, you will pass the Giant Tree and the Flatiron Tree, which fell in 1995. The Tall

Author photo

Tree of the Rockefeller Forest is on the opposite side of the creek. The Rockefeller Forest is the largest remaining continuous old-growth, uncut, coast redwood forest and has trees that are thousands of years old.

Coast redwoods like the fog in this area. Heavy winter rain and moderate year round temperatures have allowed them to become the tallest living things on the planet. Their Latin name, *Sequoia sempervirens*, means "ever living."

The Sinkyone-Lolankok people lived here for thousands of years, but the park is named for a Prussian explorer named Alexander von Humboldt. He never visited the area.

In 1921, the Save-the-Redwoods League made its first purchase of land that would eventually become the Humboldt Park. More than 100 memorial groves have been established since then. In 1930, J.D. Rockefeller Jr. donated $2 million to purchase 10,000 acres. A lumber company had owned the land but agreed to postpone logging it until the state and the League could buy the land.

A trail through some of the giant, easily accessible trees starts from Rockefeller Avenue. You can practically drive up to these trees, and several of them are labeled with names and heights.

Scientists continue to study the trees here to figure out how the anatomy of these giant trees functions when a tree grows more than 350 feet into the sky. The forest is so thick that even on brightly sunny days it is dark under the canopy.

The age of the trees, along with the serene setting, offer a feeling of calm, especially after a day of freeway driving. Don't forget to look up. The "Tall Tree" is labeled with its height in 1957: 359 feet. At that time, nearly 50 years ago, it had a circumference of 42 feet. The "Giant Tree" is thicker and taller, but it was measured later in its life.

➥ **Directions:** The park is 45 miles south of Eureka and 20 miles north of Garberville off U.S. Highway 101. The visitor's center is located two miles south of Weott on the Avenue of the Giants. The park is open year round and visitor center summer hours are from 9 A.M. to 5 P.M. daily. For more information, visit www.humboldtredwoods.org or call 707-946-2409.

Largest Monopoly Board
San Jose, CA

As they say in San Jose, "Now everyone has the chance to make it big in Silicon Valley real estate." In the middle of a park, this giant Monopoly board could hold the footprint of a small house.

Author photo

Monopoly in the Park was opened in 2002 by Friends of San Jose Beautiful, a non-profit organization that works to improve San Jose through education and empowerment.

Along with the 930 square-foot board on the ground, you can get your hands on giant dice and tokens that you wear on your head. You have to reserve that stuff in advance and there is a fee. The park uses volunteers who serve as banker, announcer, and coordinator (keeps track of whose turn it is).

The big game was made by San Jose's Cypress Granite and Memorials as an exhibit for a San Francisco design show in 1992. San Jose Beautiful installed it in San Jose's downtown Guadalupe River Park. For $300, you can rent the space and get giant dice and giant tokens. Your fee includes four hours of board time, three docents who help with the banking and rules, and the use of the tokens and giant dice. You could probably also bring your own regular-sized Monopoly pieces, but we forgot ours so just made up a game with the change in our pockets. It wasn't as fun as Monopoly, but it didn't take as long either.

➤ **Directions:** From Route 87/Guadalupe Parkway, exit at Park Avenue. Go left at Park Avenue and Right at Woz Way. The board is in the park next to the Children's Discovery Museum. For more information, visit www.monopolyinthepark.com or call 408-995-MITP.

Largest Wind Farm
San Gorgonio Pass, CA

Wind farms are clusters of wind mills grouped together to generate electricity. Several large wind farms have been set up in California; each has thousands of turbines. The fields of windmills are an amazing sight from the California freeways. Three big ones are at Altamont Pass, east of San Francisco, in the Tehachapi Mountains in Kern County and in San Gorgonio Pass, north of Palm Springs. The Department of Energy says that the Great Plains states have much more potential for wind energy than California. Energy experts say you need 14 mph average winds to produce electricity economically. But California is popular for these ventures because so many people live here and they all need electricity. Furthermore, wind farms were set up in the 1980s when the state of California required electric companies to purchase electricity from wind farms.

➤ **Directions:** You can see the turbines at Altamont Pass, from Interstate 580, between Dublin and Tracy.

Big Donut
Inglewood, CA

Mmm, a giant donut . . . and Randy's Donuts is open 24 hours! You'd be surprised what a coconut donut and a coffee can do for you when you've been driving for 12 hours and you still have two more hours between you and your mom's house in San Diego. I recommend the coconut. Don't expect anything fancy here; it's strictly donuts and a couple different beverages. There isn't even a chair to sit on, but a nice little counter lines the outside of the building.

The donut in Randy's has been around since 1952 when it was built as part of the Big Donut Drive-In chain. Since then, it's been seen in movies such as *Earth Girls Are Easy* and *Mars Attacks!*

➤ **Directions:** Randy's is close to the Los Angeles airport in Inglewood. From Highway 405, exit at Manchester Avenue. The address is 805 W. Manchester Avenue. For more information, visit www.randysdonuts.com or call 310-645-4707.

Author photo

Largest Granite Face
Yosemite National Park, CA

El Capitan is a rock-climbing favorite—a gigantic slab of rock where you can pretend you have supernatural powers to climb like a comic strip character (except you have a harness and ropes instead of spider webs on your wrists). The monolith rises almost 3,000 feet about the valley floor.

Granite makes up most of the bedrock of the Sierra Nevada mountain range. Basically, granite is igneous rock with a salt-and-pepper look due to the distribution of light and dark materials.

People have parachuted from the top of El Capitan—not all of them successfully. Base jumping from the point is illegal. Hiking and climbing is allowed.

Almost 95 percent of the park is designated wilderness, so there is a lot to explore. The Yosemite Valley has some of the most popular trails, including one to the top of El Capitan. If you are up for the challenge, expect a strenuous hike up steep terrain and the possibility of swiftly changing weather. From the Yosemite Falls trail, the top of El Capitan is 7.9 miles. There are other trail options.

➡ **Directions:** Yosemite National Park is 150 miles east of San Francisco. California State Highways 120, 140, and 41 enter the park. Entrance fees for Yosemite National Park are $20 for one vehicle for seven days. For more information, visit www.nps.gov/yose/ or call 209-372-0200.

Largest Natural Outdoor Amphitheater
Hollywood, CA

The Hollywood Bowl opened in 1922, for music under the stars and a seating capacity of just under 18,000. The Bowl is the home of the Los Angeles Philharmonic, but other performances have included a wide spectrum of greats, from the Beatles to Frank Sinatra, Ella Fitzgerald, Mariachis bands, and the rock band, Rush.

You can get a three-course "gourmet picnic box" to eat before the show. But it's not all about music. Hollywood High School has had its graduation ceremonies here.

The fountain statues at the Highland entrance were sculpted by George Stanley, the same man who designed the Oscar statue. The figures are the muses of music, drama, and dance.

➡ **Directions:** The Hollywood Bowl is located at 2301 N. Highland Avenue in Hollywood, just off the 101/Hollywood Freeway. Exit at Highland. If you can't catch a show, they have a Bowl museum, open every night before concerts. During summer months, generally from late June to mid-September, hours are 10 A.M. to show time Tuesdays through Saturdays. On Sundays, the museum is open from 4 P.M. to showtime. Off season, from mid-September to late June, the museum is open from 10 A.M. to 4:30 P.M. Admission is free. There's also a Bowl Walk, a self-guided tour around the park that points out Bowl culture, history, and architecture. Get a map online or at the Visitor's Center. For more information, visit www.hollywoodbowl.com or call 323-850-2000.

Lowest Point in the Western Hemisphere
Death Valley, CA

Weather happens in superlatives in Death Valley. It is one of the hottest places in the country and has the lowest amount of rainfall in North America; the average rainfall is less than two inches per year. Furthermore, it is the lowest point in the Western Hemisphere.

Badwater Basin is the lowest point, at 282 feet below sea level. Other names in the park are Devil's Golf Course and Funeral Peak. Makes you thirsty just thinking about it! Still, it's a national park, and more than one million annual visitors find many good reasons to hang out here.

Inside the park are ghost towns that act as outdoor museums. The land has colorful badlands, sand dunes, and even snow-covered peaks. Death Valley is a 156-mile long north-south valley through two mountain ranges: the Amargosa on the east side and the Panamint Range on the west. The forces that created a giant valley in the middle are within the earth. The tectonic plates have uplifted the mountains and sunk the valleys. The highest peak in the park, Telescope Peak, is 11,049 feet above sea level and only 15 miles from Badwater Basin.

➡ **Directions:** Death Valley National Park is along the California/Nevada border. There are two visitor centers in the park. One is in the town of Beatty, Nevada on one of the eastern portals to the park. The other is located in the Furnace Creek resort area on California Highway 190. Both are open year round. For more information, visit www.nps.gov/deva or call 760-786-3200.

Biggest Fake Dinosaurs
Cabazon, CA

Made famous in *Pee Wee's Big Adventure*, for decades the dinosaurs off Interstate 10 have welcomed many a weary traveler emerging from the desert. There's a gift shop in the belly.

➡ **Directions:** The dinosaurs are just off Interstate 10 at the Cabazon exit, west of Palm Springs.

Biggest Olive
Lindsay, CA

It's big. It's black. And it's pitted. A giant black olive stands outside the Olive Tree Inn. The concrete beauty was built to honor the local olive industry and Lindsay Ripe Olive Co., once the town's largest employer.

➡ **Directions:** Lindsay is southeast of Fresno. From Interstate 5, head east on State Route 137 into town. The big olive is located outside the Olive Tree Inn at 390 N. Highway 65.

Biggest Box of Raisins
Kingsburg, CA

In 1992, Fresno State University students built a monument to their local raisin industry with a giant red box of Sun-Maid raisins. It was once filled with raisins, but now you have to go inside the store here to get a handful.

The Sun-Maid cooperative dates back to 1912 when a group of raisin growers proposed a grower-owned agency to help spread the word about the greatness of raisins. The original Sun-Maid girl, Lorraine Collett, was a raisin packer when she was chosen for the job. She posed in 1915 for the trademark image that is still recognized around the world. At one point, she was part of a marketing promotion that had her flying in a plane over San Francisco dropping raisins on people. According to Sun-Maid, today their processing facility covers 130 acres; more than 75 percent of California's raisin crop grows within 25 miles of the Kingsburg plant.

It takes more than four pounds of grapes to make a pound of raisins. The grapes are usually picked in August and dried out in the sun for two to three weeks to get to raisin form.

➡ **Directions:** Kingsburg is roughly 20 miles southeast of Fresno at 13525 S. Bethel Avenue. From State Highway 99, watch signs for

Bethel Avenue. The Sun-Maid growers store is located on the east side of the freeway. The box is located outside, but doesn't have raisins in it anymore. Hours are 8:30 A.M. to 5 P.M. Monday through Friday and from 9:30 A.M. to 5 P.M. on Saturday. For more information, visit www.sunmaid.com or call 800-786-6243.

Biggest Artichoke
Castroville, CA

It's so authentic, this giant artichoke even has spiky tips. It was built in 1972, is 20 feet tall and 15 feet wide. The town has a yearly artichoke festival, usually in May that features an artichoke eating festival and "Agroart," where you sculpt fruit and vegetables. You can even tour an artichoke field!

➤ **Directions:** The giant artichoke is located at the Giant Artichoke Restaurant in Castroville, a coastal town in between Monterey and Santa Cruz. The restaurant is located at 11261 Merritt Street. For more information on the area, visit www.artichoke-festival.org.

COLORADO

Tallest Sand Dune Field
Great Sand Dunes National Park Area, CO

Between two bold mountain ranges, this expanse of sand looks completely out of place. Usually you see these rolling fields of sand in the desert or on the beach. Here in Western Colorado, you can see them from miles away, a tan-colored mound piled right up next to green mountains.

The dunes are in a high altitude area of the San Luis Valley of the Rockies. They cover 30 square miles and have been as high as 750 feet tall. Billions of grains of sand make up the dunes. These tiny particles have blown in from the San Juan and Sangre de Cristo mountains, leaving them here at the base. The rivers and streams from the mountain ranges have left behind sand particles as well.

If it's windy, consider wearing pants because the blowing sand can bite at your legs. People walk around in an Arabian like scene with scarves covering their heads to protect them from the sand. You might see people walking up the hills with sleds and kites, but the climb is deceptive. You slide with every step, so it takes longer to walk than you first might think. Take along a snack and water to stay hydrated.

Consider wearing sport sandals to cross the trickling stream that abuts the dunes. Tennis shoes quickly fill with sand.

➤ **Directions:** The visitor center is accessible from Highway 150. Admission is $3. The visitor center is open year round with longer hours during the summer. From Memorial Day to Labor Day, hours are 9 A.M. to 7 P.M. For more information, visit www.nps.gov/grsa or call 719-378-6399.

Highest Bridge
Royal Gorge, CO

Warning: this site is not for those wary of heights. The bridge crossing the Royal Gorge is truly amazing. It was built as a tourist attraction in 1929 and it still draws people here. There is no other reason to cross it, because the bridge doesn't really lead anywhere except in a loop back to the same highway.

The bridge rises 1,053 feet over the Arkansas River, where you can see river rafters gliding below. The bridge itself is accessible to cars and pedestrians—you can debate which is more unnerving. The base of the bridge is made of more than 1,000 wooden planks which clank when cars drive over them. On foot, through the cracks, you can see the river below. On a windy day, the flags on the bridge flap in the breeze.

The bridge cost $250,000 to build. A 22 minute film tells a bit of the history of the bridge and the park.

The building began with the construction of concrete abutments to serve as the bases for the steel towers. The bases were made out of crushed rock from granite excavated from the canyon rim. Roughly 80 men were employed at the height of construction. Some lived in a boarding house on the south side of the canyon, while others commuted from Canon City.

Gusting winds were a threat to safety, and some crew members had near misses. After the towers were constructed, wires were strung across the canyon one at a time. More than 1,000 tons of structural steel was used to make the bridge. Crews worked from both sides. The final work included laying the wooden deck and fastening the ends of roughly 1,300 planks to the sides of the bridge. The work was completed within six months with no major accidents.

The bridge was refurbished in 1984, and it remains in operation today. The gorge, however, continues to change, with water and sand slowly digging the canyon deeper.

Near the bridge is an amusement park of features. There's bungee jumping, a movie theater on history, and even live music and live bison. You pay for it with the price of admission. It's $20 even if you just want to cross the bridge. You can get a $7 refund if you leave the park within an hour of entering.

➥ **Directions:** The bridge is located 12 miles west of Canon City on U.S. Highway 50. You can get to the bridge on 3A from two exits off Highway 50, but the entrance closer to Canon City is much faster. From the west entrance, the bridge is seven miles. From the east entrance, (the one closer to Canon City) it's five miles and the road is in better shape. From the west entrance, 3A has no shoulder in spots and weak dividing lines. The two entrances basically form a loop with the bridge in between. Campers are not allowed on the bridge, but there are parking lots on either side. The bridge is open from 10:30 A.M. to 6 P.M. For more information, visit www.royalgorgebridge.com or call 888-333-5597.

Most Secure Prison
Florence, CO

There are no tours at the United States Penitentiary, so unless you feel like committing a serious crime, you're not going to get in. Don't take any photos, and don't linger for too long (not that you'd want to.) Drive past just quickly enough to ponder crime and punishment. And don't be fooled by a couple of other prisons in the area. We passed two on our way to this one.

Several public enemies live or have lived here. Timothy McVeigh spent time here for the 1995 bombing of the Alfred P. Murrah Federal Building in Oklahoma City, which killed 168 people and injured dozens more. McVeigh was eventually taken to Indiana for his execution in 2001, where he died of lethal injection. Ted Kaczynski is here serving a life sentence without parole. Kaczynski mailed bombs to people whom he thought perpetuated evil through technological progress. He himself had a doctorate in mathematics from the University of Michigan and taught at UC Berkeley. His bombs killed three people and injured 29 more, including professors. More recently, many of the worst of the newer terrorists, once caught, have been brought here.

➤ **Directions:** The Supermax is just outside Florence. From 115, go south on Highway 67. You're not supposed to take photos.

Giant Rocking Chair
Penrose, CO

There are other large rockers out there, but we're not sure you can get lemonade and homemade pie while you're visiting them. (Texas, home of many big things, has the largest cedar rocker at the Texas Hill Country Furniture and Mercantile store in Lipan. The store is five miles south of the 281/120 intersection.) But as far as we can tell, this rocker in Colorado might be the heaviest. Tom and Carole Doxey bought it just to put it out front of their shop in Penrose. He needed a tractor trailer to move it here.

Author photo

It was originally made for a furniture shop, but Tom had his eye on it for his store, Doxey's Apple Shed Mercantile. Now it sits out front attracting guests. His old building used to be an apple warehouse, and the interior is worth visiting (if not for the homemade food) for the brick interior and tall ceilings. Local schools used the warehouse for basketball 50 years ago and their initials are still carved into the rails.

Today they sell everything from landscape supplies to homemade pastries.

➤ **Directions:** The Rocking Chair is outside on Highway 115, just north of Highway 50 on the east side of 115.

Highest Paved Road
Mt. Evans Scenic Byway, CO

This road rises from 7,500 feet to 14,000 feet above sea level in 28 miles. On a clear day, the view stretches from the great plains of Colorado to the other peaks in the Colorado Rockies. Along the route are trails, picnic areas, high alpine lakes, permafrost, and bighorn sheep.

You will pass Echo Lake at 10,600 feet; Lincoln Lake at 11,700 feet and Summit Lake at 12,830 feet. More than 100 trails on the mountain take you away from the road and closer to the lakes, views, and forests. In the 1940s, a restaurant was built at the top, but it burned down in 1979. It was never rebuilt, but the foundation remains.

➤ **Directions:** There is a charge of $10 to drive up the road. The road is open 24 hours a day seasonally. It typically opens for the summer season around Memorial Day and closes around Labor Day. From Interstate 70, take exit 240 in Idaho Springs. Follow Highway 103 south until it meets Echo Lake. Take Highway 5 to the top of Mt. Evans. There is a parking area, and then a quarter-mile walk to the top. For more information, visit www.mountevans.com or call 303-567-3000.

Largest Mural
Pueblo, CO

The Pueblo Levee Project mural is nearly two miles long, stretched out along the concrete levee along the Arkansas River in Pueblo, Colorado. The project started in 1979 with random paintings on the side of the levee, a giant concrete wall that separates the river from the city. When it was last officially measured in the mid 1990s, it was 175,000 square feet of painting.

"It's probably a lot longer than that," said Cynthia Ramu, a middle school art teacher who helps organize group paintings on the wall.

"Everything just kind of grew off of each other," said Ramu. "It's real public art." Everything is painted on a 45 degree angle. More than 1,000 artists have taken part, including groups of school kids and artists, who've come in from out of town to take part. The site encourages recycled paints, in part because one of the organizers, Dave Roberts, has worked in the state's paint recycling program. You can't just go paint part of it, though. You need a permit, or else it's considered graffiti.

➤ **Directions:** From Interstate 25, exit at First Street. Turn south onto Union Avenue and follow Union across the bridge. Turn right at the end of the bridge on Corona Avenue. You can park along Corona. For more information, visit www.pueblo.org.

CONNECTICUT

Largest Casino
Mashantucket, CT

You'd think Las Vegas, but no, the largest casino not just in the United States, but in the world, is Foxwoods, located on the Mashantucket Pequot Tribal Nation. The hotel has more than 1,400 rooms.

Like Vegas, and unlike other reservation casinos, you do get free alcoholic drinks here when you're gambling, and the games are pervasive. There are more than 6,000 slot machines, 350 table games, high stakes bingo, a poker room, and even a smoke-free gambling area. There are Pai Gow dominoes, baccarat, roulette, and a generous offering of high and low limit poker games. In the sports book you can bet on horses, dogs, and j'ai alai. Entertainment includes a night club, shops, 24 restaurants and performers who've included Bill Maher, Mary J. Blige, Don Henley, and the Chippendales. A few distinct differences from Vegas: windows. Unlike in Sin City, here you can actually tell whether it's day or night outside. The casino and hotel areas are decorated with Native American Art and have stores and shops such as the Rainmaker Café and Wampum Trading Post.

➨ **Directions:** From Interstates 395 or 95, access the casino via Route 2. Once you're on 2, you should see signs dotting the highway pointing the way to the casino. For more information, visit www.foxwoods.com or call 1-800-FOXWOOD.

Oldest Steam Powered Cider Mill
Old Mystic, CT

Annette Miner's great grandfather started making apple cider in 1881, and the family has been making it ever since. Miner and her husband are the fourth generation to work at the mill, and they have fifth and sixth generation family members working with them. They get most of the apples from the Hudson Valley in New York, and during the fall you can watch the conveyor roll them into the mill. Everything is run off a steam engine, which has received the designation of National Historic Mechanical Engineering Landmark.

"Everything is good solid fruit. We don't use drops," said Miner. They use 50 to 70 tons of apples per week in the fall. All of their products are sold on site.

Directions: The B.F. Clyde's Cider Mill is located at 129 N. Stonington Road in Old Mystic. From Interstate 95, take exit 90 and head north on Route 27. Keep to the right. The mill is open everyday from September 1 to New Years Eve, but they only make the cider three to five days a week. During the fall, they make cider every weekend, at least a couple times a day, so that visitors can see the process. For more information, call 860-536-3354.

Oldest Wooden Whaling Ship
Mystic, CT

Thar she blows! People who work on the Charles W. Morgan will actually yell that, and more, to show you what it was like to hunt whales out on the open sea. This is the only remaining wooden whaling ship left in the world; today it is a floating museum. Built in 1841, it sailed out on the open sea for at least 80 years. In 1941, it was donated to Mystic Seaport. Visitors can go above and below the ship and watch the "crew" climb to the top of the sails, where real seamen once sat watching for whales. Trips on the Charles W. Morgan typically lasted three to five years—and you thought you worked long hours!

Credit: Mystic Seaport

When the watchman saw a whale, crew members would jump in the smaller 30 foot boats and head out after the whales. They would harpoon the whale and possibly get a "Nantucket sleigh ride," where the small boat is pulled by the whale. Then they'd row the whale back toward the ship and "peel the blubber like an orange," said Michael O'Farrell, the publicist at Mystic Seaport. They'd leave the carcass behind and use the blubber for oil.

"They would go home when the boat was full of oil," O'Farrell said. Huge pots for converting blubber into whale oil are forward on the boat; quarters for officers and men are below.

The ship has sailed in every ocean, O'Farrell said. Since the boat has been in the sea and it's made of wood, it has had been restored quite a bit. To date, it has roughly 30 percent of its original 1841 timber.

Directions: Mystic Seaport is roughly 10 miles east of New London in southeastern Connecticut. From Interstate 95, take exit 90. Turn left at the end of the ramp and head south on Route 27 for one mile. Mystic Seaport parking lot is the second lot on the left. Admission is $17 for adults and $9 for children who are six to twelve years of age. Admission is cheaper in the winter. The museum is open everyday but Dec. 25. From April through October, hours are 9 A.M. to 5 P.M. For more information, visit www.mysticseaport.org or call 888-9-SEAPORT.

WASHINGTON, D.C.

Largest Library
Washington, D.C

The Library of Congress is the largest library in the world, with nearly 128 million items on more than 530 miles of bookshelves. That's a lot of Dewey Decimals. According to the library, the institution serves as the research arm for the U.S. Congress but also is the oldest federal cultural institution in the nation. The collection includes 29 million books, 2.7 million recordings, 12 million photographs, 4.8 million maps and 57 million manuscripts. But no, they don't have a copy of everything printed in the country. All the stuff is stacked on shelves in three different buildings. The stacks are closed to the public, but visitors can see the Main Reading Room and the Great Hall from the visitor's gallery.

They've even got a Librarian of Congress who is appointed by the President and approved by the Senate. There have been 13 librarians, including the current librarian, James Billington, who was appointed to the job by Ronald Reagan in 1987. But of course the burning question on many a reader's mind: can you get a library card? Yes, but you can't check out books. The Library of Congress is strictly a research library, so books can only be used on the premises—kind of like one giant reference section. Anyone older than 18 who wants to use the reading room or collections must have a "Reader Identification" card. User cards are available at the reader registration station in Room LM140 of the Madison building. You do your own research online or in card catalogs and then give a call slip to a researcher who retrieves the material for you.

There's a lot to see here! Thomas Jefferson's personal library is considered the core of the whole place; he is considered the library's champion. His personal library is part of the Rare Book and Special Collections Division. The library was founded in 1800. It was housed in a boarding house and in the Capitol before the Thomas Jefferson Building was built in 1897. The John Adams Building opened in 1939 and the James Madison Memorial Building opened in 1980. Apart from standard materials, the Copyright Office is also located here on the fourth floor of the Madison building.

Directions: The Library of Congress is located at 101 Independence Ave, SE, on the east side of the U.S. Capitol. The closest metro stop is Capitol South. The library hours vary by building. The Thomas Jefferson Building, where the visitor's center is located, is open from 10 A.M. to 5:30 P.M. Monday through Saturday. For more information, visit www.loc.gov or call 202-707-8000.

Most Popular Museum
Washington, D.C.

The National Air and Space Museum claims the title as most popular museum. It is part of the Smithsonian Institution, which is in many ways a giant concentration of superlatives. The Smithsonian is the largest museum in the world with 16 museums, a zoo, and more than 140 million items. The National Air and Space Museum is the most popular, because it has recorded the highest daily attendance of any museum (more than

100,000 people in one day). According to the Smithsonian, more than nine million people visit the museum every year.

Inside the museum are twenty-three galleries explaining everything from early balloon flights to space travel. You can see the original 1903 Wright Flyer and the Apollo 11 command module *Columbia*, which went to the moon in 1969.

Only ten percent of the Smithsonian's air and space collection is displayed at the building on the National Mall. At the new Udvar-Hazy Center in Chantilly, Virginia, (near Dulles Airport) you can see the world's fastest jet, the Lockheed SR-71 Blackbird. Also here is the *Enola Gay*, which dropped the first atomic bomb during World War II.

➡ **Directions:** Smithsonian museums are free. The new Udvar-Hazy Center opened in December 2003; there are shuttles to and from the mall for $7. The National Air and space Museum is located at Independence Avenue at 4th Street, SW on the National Mall. The hours are 10 A.M. to 5:30 P.M. everyday except December 25th. For more information, visit www.nasm.si.edu or call 202-633-1000.

Largest Administration Building
Arlington, VA

According to U.S. Department of Defense statistics, the Pentagon building easily trumps other administration buildings in the country, in terms of size. The Pentagon has three times the amount of floor space as the Empire State Building in New York. The U.S. Capitol could fit inside one of the five wedge-shaped sections.

This is just a slice of the national government. The building has 23,000 employees, civilian and military, working to protect national interests. There are 16 parking lots, 131 stairways, 4,200 clocks and 691 drinking fountains. They even have a Defense Post Office that handles more than one million pieces of mail every month. Despite 17 miles of corridors, they say it only takes seven minutes to walk between any two points in the building.

The original site for the building was known as Arlington Farms. It was bordered by five roads that compelled the design of the five-sided pentagon shaped building. President Franklin D. Roosevelt didn't want the building to distract from the D.C. skyline or from Arlington National Cemetery, so he asked that the building be moved three quarters of a mile down river.

The style is Stripped Neo-Classical. The building was constructed of reinforced concrete made from sand dredged from the Potomac River. Three shifts worked 24 hours a day, seven days a week, for 18 months to get the building finished. The wedges were occupied as they were finished. The building is 6.6 million square feet.

The idea behind the Pentagon was born in 1941 when the War Department decided to do something about its lack of space. The first occupants moved in April 1942.

Directions: The Pentagon is located in Arlington, Virginia, just off Interstate 395 on the Virginia side of the Potomac River. Exit at Pentagon South Parking. You can also take the Metro Blue Line to the Pentagon station. Tours are available to select groups such as schools and educational organizations by reservation only. For more information, visit www.defenselink.mil/pubs/pentagon/ or call 703-697-1776.

Tallest Obelisk
Washington, D.C.

The Washington Monument towers over Washington and is the largest obelisk in the world. George Washington died in 1799. Immediately monuments around the country went up to honor the nation's first president. For awhile, folks in Washington, D.C. wanted to build a big pyramid for George Washington, and bury him underneath. (The House liked the idea but the Senate didn't) The obelisk that was built is not too far off the Egyptian idea of a pyramid, but this American obelisk towers over anything along the Nile. The Washington Monument is taller than even the highest steps of the biggest Egyptian pyramid.

The Washington Monument is 555 feet tall. Its exterior is made from white marble, primarily from Baltimore. The interior is granite from Maine.

The Washington National Monument Society held a competition in 1836 to try and find a fitting memorial. The winning design went to Robert Mills, who went on to work on other buildings in Washington, D.C. Mills' design was changed significantly before the monument was completed.

His idea was to build a rotunda with 30 massive columns and statues of the signers of the Declaration of Independence. In the center would be a 600-foot tall four-sided obelisk. It wasn't until 1848 that Congress granted a site to the Society for the monument. It was the site that L'Enfant had planned for the memorial, but soil tests showed that the site was too marshy, so it had to be moved 100 yards to the Southeast. This move disrupts the alignment with the Capitol and the White House with the planned axis.

The cornerstone was put down in 1848. There was a parade to the site and railroad fares were reduced to mark the event. School kids were asked to donate a penny to help fund the construction. By 1854, the obelisk was 152 feet tall.

When the Society ran low on resources, the states were asked for donations. Alabama said it could donate some stone. The Society liked the idea and soon asked other states and foreign countries to donate blocks of marble or stone for the monument. Pope Pius IX gave a block of marble. The stone was stolen, possibly by a group who didn't like the Catholic Church and swore that the stone would never be part of the monument. (Many others donated stones; 193 memorial stones adorn the east and west interior walls but they are no longer accessible to the public for "security and resource protection," according to the Park Service). At the start of the Civil War, the monument was 176 feet tall.

As the nation's 100 year anniversary approached, members of government hoped to get the monument completed. But there was worry over the stability of the foundation, which some believed wasn't strong enough to hold up such a huge monument.

Studies were done of the soil and of Egyptian obelisks to determine a modified scope, size and dimensions. The nine-inch pyramid of cast aluminum was placed on top on 1884. It was opened to the public in 1888—eighy-nine years after Washington's death.

➡ **Directions:** The Washington Monument is located at Constitution Avenue and 15th Street in Washington. It is open every day except December 25 from 9 A.M. to 5 P.M. Like some of the other popular public buildings in D.C., there are a limited number of tickets distributed daily, so plan accordingly. Free tickets are distributed at the ticket kiosk starting at 8 A.M. For more information, visit www.nsp.gov/wash/ or call 202-426-6841.

FLORIDA

Biggest Door
Cape Canaveral, FL

The vehicle assembly building at Cape Canaveral has doors that are so big a space ship can fit through them. Visitors can't go in it, since the government is making space shuttles inside, but you can see the building and its giant doors from the outside when you're on a tour. The Kennedy Space Center is loaded with active and legendary space items.

Credit: NASA

➡ **Directions:** The Kennedy Space Center Visitor Complex is located on State Road 405, six miles inside the Kennedy Space Center entrance. From I-95, take exit 78 northbound or 79 southbound. The center is opened daily from 9 A.M. to dusk everyday except December 25 and certain launch days. The priciest, most inclusive admission ticket is $35 for adults and $25 for children ages 3 to 11. For more information, visit www.kennedyspacecenter.com or call 321-449-4444.

Smallest Post Office
Ochopee, FL

The structure is 62 square feet, according to the postal service, and looks about the size of a kid's playhouse in the middle of the Big Cypress National Preserve east of Naples.

According to the Collier County historical marker on site, the building used to be an irrigation pipe shed used by a tomato farm. After a fire in 1953 destroyed the Ochopee general store, where the post office was located, the shed was quickly converted into the post office that remains today. The office handles mail for a three county area that stretches more than 100 miles, including delivery to members of the Seminole and Miccosukee tribes who live nearby.

➤ **Directions:** The post office is on the south side of U.S. 41 The post office is open from 9:30 A.M. to noon and 1 P.M. to 4:30 P.M. Monday through Friday. On Saturdays, it's open from 9:30 A.M. to 11:30 A.M.

Largest Religious Theme Park
Orlando, FL

If you don't have time to get to Jerusalem, the folks at the Holy Land Experience hope to offer you the next best thing. "It's been 2,000 years since the world has seen anything like this!" according to their press materials. And they may be right.

The complex is a $16 million, 15-acre museum dedicated to Jerusalem. The facility opened in 2001 and was created by a non-profit group called Zion's Hope, a Christian ministry and educational organization. In the park is a replica of the tomb where Jesus was buried and the world's largest indoor model of the city of Jerusalem. Actors play out biblical stories. A museum has scrolls, bibles, manuscripts, and other artifacts. In the Oasis Palms Café you can get a Goliath Burger or a Bedouin beef sandwich.

➤ **Directions:** The Holy Land Experience is located in Orlando off Interstate 4 at exit 78, at the corner of Conroy and Vineland roads. For more information, visit www.theholylandexperience.com or call 866-USA-Holy.

GEORGIA

Largest Stone Sculpture
Stone Mountain, GA

The mounted figures of Jefferson Davis, Robert E. Lee and Thomas "Stonewall" Jackson grace the side of a mountain near Atlanta; these are Confederate heroes of the Civil War. Together they form Stone Mountain, the largest stone sculpture in the country. Davis was the first and only president of the Confederate States of America from 1861 to 1865. Lee was a Confederate general during the Civil War. Jackson was a Confederate commander.

Owners of the mountain, the Venable family, deeded the north face of the mountain to the United Daughters of the Confederacy in 1916. The UDC was given 12 years to complete a Civil War monument, according to the park history. The memorial took quite a bit longer.

Three sculptors worked on the carving during its creation. The first, Gutzon Borglum, went on to carve Mt. Rushmore. Borglum was hired in 1915 and completed the head of Lee in 1924. He left the project before finishing because of a disagreement with management.

The second sculptor, Augustus Lukeman, took over in 1925. Lukeman removed Borglum's work from the mountain, but by 1928 the only thing he had created was another head of Lee. The Venable family took their property back and the mountain was uncarved for the next 36 years.

The state of Georgia bought the mountain and surrounding land in 1958, and five years later, a new sculptor was chosen to do the job. Walter Kirtland Hancock was the man, and it would take him until 1972 to complete the biggest stone sculpture in the world. He used thermo-jet torches to carve away the granite.

The entire carved surface covers three acres and is 90 feet high. The carving is recessed 42 feet into the mountain. A 3,200-acre park surrounds the monolith. There are hiking and bike trails, tennis, golf, and even laser shows.

➤ **Directions:** Stone Mountain Park is located 16 miles east of downtown Atlanta on Highway 78. Entrance to Stone Mountain Park requires a $7 one day permit per vehicle. For more information, visit www.stonemountainpark.com or call 770-498-5690.

Largest Peanut
Ashburn, GA

The giant peanut of Ashburn, Georgia rises from the landscape like a king wearing his crown at his feet. The Turner Chamber of Commerce will tell you that communities were built around agriculture and the peanut trade played a large part in feeding the farmers around here. In honor of that role, one Ashburn resident built a monument to the crop in 1975. It is 20 feet tall. According to the Peanut Advisory Board, Georgia is the country's largest producer of peanuts, producing 41 percent of the U.S. crop. The Golden Peanut Company has a peanut processing plant in the city. Some say it's the world's largest.

➤ **Directions:** The giant peanut can be seen from Interstate 75, roughly a half mile south of exit 28.

Biggest Apple
Cornelia, GA

You can keep a lot of doctors away with this baby. The Big Red Apple was dedicated in 1926 as a shrine to the area's apple industry. An Apple Queen and court were on hand for the festivities. According to Cornelia City Hall, the monument was donated by Southern Railway for the annual apple celebration. It is seven feet tall and has a circumference of 22 feet. Weighing in at 5,200 pounds, it has enough nutrients to fuel several schools worth of children through their elementary years. If only it weren't made of steel and concrete. . . . The Big Red Apple festival continues every year in Cornelia in October.

➨ **Directions:** The big apple is located at the railroad train depot, 107 Clarksville Street. For more information, visit www.habershamchamber.com.

HAWAII

Largest Hedge Maze
Wahiawa, Oahu, HI

Aloha and mahalo for this glorious shrine to all things pineapple at the Dole Pineapple Plantation. The pineapple garden maze covers more than two acres with a path inside of 1.7 miles. The hedge of no end is made up of 11,000 plants. From the air, you can see a giant pineapple in the middle of the maze. If you get out successfully, you can get a coupon worth 15 percent off any retail item at the Dole Plantation!

Pineapples are big in Hawaii, but not native. People think they originated in Paraguay and were traded around the world, eventually landing in Hawaii in the 1500s. The Dole Plantation was once a fruit stand.

➨ **Directions:** The Dole Plantation is located near Wahiawa in central Oahu and is open from 9 A.M. to 5:30 P.M. daily. Take H-2 north to Kamehameha Highway/99 to 64-1550 Kamehameha Highway. The maze costs $5 for adults and $3 for children. For more information, visit www.dole-plantation.com or call 808-621-8408.

Largest Observatory
Mauna Kea, Big Island, HI

The top of Mauna Kea, Hawaii's highest mountain, is home to 11 internationally sponsored telescopes, including two of the largest telescopes in

Credit: Hawai'i Convention and Visitors Bureau

operation. There are two Keck Telescopes—the world's largest optical and infrared telescopes—located here. Each is eight stories tall and weighs 300 tons. Their primary mirrors are more than 30 feet in diameter.

With the telescopes, astrophysicists seek answers to some of the most complex questions facing the human race, including the evolution of the universe. The first telescope started operating on Mauna Kea in 1992 and the second in 1996. The observatory is operated by the California Institute of Technology, the University of California, and NASA. The observatory's location is good for major telescopes because it's high enough to get away from some of the earth's atmosphere. The air is calm and the sky is dark. Furthermore, the mountain is usually above the cloud line.

➤ **Directions:** The Keck Observatory doesn't provide tours but does have a visitor's gallery with a video, information on the observatory and science, and a viewing area where you can see some of the Keck I telescope. The gallery is open from 10 A.M. to 4 P.M. Monday through Friday. The University of Hawaii manages the 11,600 acre science reserve at the summit and offers weekend tours at the Onizuka Visitor's Center at 9,200 feet. For more information, visit www2.keck.hawaii.edu or call 808-961-2180.

Tallest Sea Cliffs
Molokai, HI

The sea cliffs along the north coast of Hawaii are the highest in the world. They rise 3,000 feet above sea level. The island was formed by two volcanoes, and the cliffs were formed as a result of a huge landslide a million years ago. Geologists have said that the landslide was so powerful it caused a tsunami on the neighboring island of Lanai. They also say the landscape is still changing. In 1999, a landslide near Pelekunu Valley carried enough debris into the ocean to create six acres of new land.

Directions: You can see the Molokai sea cliffs from air, sea or land. At Pala'au State Park, at the end of the Kale Highway/47, you can see a scenic overlook of Kalalupapa, the peninsula where people with leprosy were once banished.

Most Active Volcano
Kilauea, Big Island, HI

Not only does the big island of Hawaii have the most massive volcano, Mauna Loa, but it also has the most active. It's not everyday you can see burning red mounds of liquid earth flowing into the sea. This is pretty cool stuff.

According to the U.S. Geological Survey, the volcano formed between 300,000 and 600,000 years ago. It's been active in some form or another ever since. Kilauea's current eruption began in January 1983 and was still going at press time. The U.S. Geological Survey posts a lava flow update regularly at the Hawaii Volcanoes Web site. This eruption is called the Pu'u'O'o-Kapaianaha eruption and is thought to be the longest rift-zone eruption in more than 600 years.

In the early years of the eruption, the earth spit lava fountains 1,500 feet into the air. But it's not just an interesting site for tourists. Locals have had to adapt to the changing landscape. Since 1983, lava flow has covered at least eight miles of highway and destroyed nearly 200 structures. Flows in 1990 covered the village of Kalapana. Kilauea is the youngest volcano on the Hawaiian Islands.

Lava is still flowing into the ocean, where you can watch it from a safe distance, at the end of the Chain of Craters Road. There's a one hour hike (one-way) at the end of the road. (The hazards of the area include volcanic fumes, methane gas explosions and coastline collapse, so heed all posted warnings seriously. People have died and disappeared by crossing over into roped off areas.) The National Park here encompasses more than 10 percent of the island.

➤ **Directions:** Highway 11 leads to the Hawaii Volcano National Park on the big island of Hawaii, 30 miles from Hilo. The park is open 24 hours a day, every day. The visitor's center is open from 7:45 A.M. to 5 P.M. daily. The entrance fee is $10 per vehicle. For more information, visit http://hvo.wr.usgs.gov or call 808-985-6000 for the eruption update recorded message.

IDAHO

Biggest Baked Potato
Blackfoot, ID

Where else but Idaho would you find a giant potato? Out from of the Idaho Potato Expo, you can see a brown giant. Here at the Expo, as they say, "We give tators to Out-of-Staters."

Here you can see the history of the potato in all of its glory that led up to the ultimate honor of an Idaho license plate designation. Inside you can learn interesting facts, such as: Did you know the potato is 80 percent water? There's also a giant potato chip to see.

➤ **Directions:** The Potato Expo is located at 130 NW Main Street. Admission is $3 for adults and $1 for children ages 6 to 12, but the giant baked potato is outside the main entrance. The museum is open year round with summer hours of 9:30 A.M. to 5 P.M. Monday through Saturday. For more information, visit www.potatoexpo.com or call 208-785-2517.

Deepest River Gorge
Hell's Canyon, ID

Slicing the border between Idaho and Oregon, Hell's Canyon is the deepest river gorge in the country. The canyon was carved by the Snake River and at one point, the river is 8,000 feet below Oregon's west rim. Roughly seven miles down from Hell's Canyon Dam, the river elevation is 1,480 feet. The canyon depth here is 7,913 feet—even higher than the

Grand Canyon's north rim. Overhead is Idaho's Seven Devils range at 9,393 feet.

The canyon is the result of millions of years of the earth's movements and changes. In the cliffs above the river is evidence of volcanic activity from more than 100 million years ago. Hell's Canyon was formed as the Snake River has cut its way through a rising mountain range over the past two million years. The cutting power was increased by water from melting glaciers and rainfall.

The gorge is covered by the Hell's Canyon National Recreation Area, which protects more than 650,000 acres. Just over 67 miles of the Snake River is within the recreation area. Because of the wide variation in elevation, you can find both desert landscapes and alpine lakes here. The area is largely undeveloped, with no roads going all the way across, so it's smart to have a map. You can order and look at them online.

➨ **Directions:** A good lookout point into the canyon is at Hat Point Lookout, the highest point on the Oregon rim. Here you can see the canyon from 6,982 feet. Hat Point Lookout is located 23 miles from Imhaha on Forest Roads 4240 and 315. The road is open from July to November and is not recommended for trailers. For more information, go to the Wallowa Mountains Visitor Center in Enterprise, Oregon, visit www.fs.fed.us/hellscanyon, or call 541-426-5546.

Largest Concentration of Horse Fossils
Hagerman, ID

The Smithsonian found hundreds of specimens of an extinct horse here—so many that they call it a horse quarry. The site was 5,000 square feet and filled with so many different animal parts, scientists believe there was probably a watering hole nearby. The extinct horse existed 3.5 million years ago and today is known as the Hagerman. He's the earliest known representative of what would become the standard horse we know and love today. The Hagerman was about the same size as the modern day zebra. He eventually evolved into the modern horse; but about 10,000 years ago, the horse in North America disappeared altogether. The cause is unknown, but theories include a climactic catastrophe or prehistoric humans relying on the horse for food. The horse wasn't reintroduced into North America until the Spanish conquistadors brought them from Europe in the late 1500s.

At Hagerman, the geological record details what this area was once like.

People have found camel bones here. The paleontologists at Hagerman Fossil Beds say camels originated in North America and that their presence in the Middle East is recent, geologically speaking. When they lived at Hagerman, the area was lush, not the desert it is now. Fossils of turtles, frogs, and water fowl show that the area was probably wetlands two or three million years ago.

➡ **Directions:** Hagerman Fossil Beds National Monument is open year round, with longer hours during the summer. From Memorial Day to Labor Day, the hours are 8 A.M. to 5 P.M. from Sunday to Thursday. On Friday and Saturday, the hours are 8 A.M. to 8 P.M. Closed Thanksgiving, December 25, and January 1, the park is free and located in the town of Hagerman, at 221 N. State Street. From I-84, exit at U.S. Highway 30. For more information, visit www.nps.gov/hafo/ or call 208-837-4793.

ILLINOIS

Largest Tyrannosaurus Rex Skeleton
Chicago, IL

Even without flesh, the T-rex named Sue is an awesome site. Giant claws, more than 50 huge teeth, and a head that was once as big as a refrigerator. She is 42 feet long and 12 feet tall at the hips.

She was found in South Dakota by a woman named Sue Hendrickson, hence the skeleton's name. In truth, scientists aren't sure if it's a male or female. Sue is the largest ever discovered and also the best preserved. The bones alone weigh 3,000 pounds and when it was alive, it was probably seven tons.

In 1990, Hendrickson and a team from Black Hills Institute were looking for fossils in western South Dakota. One day in August, their truck got a flat tire. Most of the team went to get it fixed, but Hendrickson stayed behind to scout around. She wandered to some sandstone bluffs that looked interesting and within minutes spotted some bones. The find turned out to be huge.

There was a court battle over who owned the bones. After several years ownership went to the land owner, who put the bones up for auction. The

Author photo

Field Museum in Chicago was the highest bidder, paying more than $8 million for the skeleton. The museum unveiled Sue in 2000.

Upstairs at the Field Museum, scientists are still working on the bones. Museum visitors can watch them scraping pinkie finger sized pieces of bone. The museum also explains theories and the many things scientists don't know about dinosaurs, like: Are birds living dinosaurs because their skeletons are similar?

Sue's skeleton is 90 percent complete. Her skull is displayed separately upstairs. The real one is too heavy to be mounted on the giant skeleton, so a cast is acting as its double.

You can see Sue from the entrance of the museum; to get close you have to pay admission. The museum had 52 free days in 2004—typically Mondays and Tuesdays during the off-season: January, February and during the fall.

➤ **Directions:** The Field Museum is located just off Lake Michigan at 1400 S. Lake Shore Drive in downtown Chicago. Admission is $17 for adults and $8 for children ages 3 to 11. Seniors and students with identification get in for $14. Chicago residents get a discount. Parking is costly around the museum ($12 at the museum campus) so consider taking a Chicago Transit Authority (CTA) train, which has a stop nearby at Roosevelt. You can walk from there or take CTA bus #6. Museum hours are 9 A.M. to 5 P.M. daily with last admission allowed at 4 P.M. For more information visit www.fieldmuseum.org or call 312-922-9410.

Tallest Building
Chicago, IL

The Sears Tower is still the tallest building in the United States. You can see it from miles away, but would you want to live all the way up there? Try it out on the observation deck of the Sears Tower; the Skydeck is 1,353 feet above ground.

The Sears Tower was the world's tallest office building until 1996 when the Petronas Towers were constructed in Kuala Lumpur, Malasia. The structures atop the Petronas towers make them taller than the Sears Tower, but the Sears still has the tallest roof and the tallest habitable floor. The distance to the top of the roof is 1,450 feet and the highest occupied floor is at 1,431 feet. The building is on two city blocks and has 110 floors. It opened in 1973 and has 4.5 million square feet of floor space.

➥ **Directions:** The Sears Tower is located at 233 S. Wacker Drive in downtown Chicago. The tower is a couple blocks from both Union Station and the Quincy train stops. You can visit the Skydeck from 10 A.M. to 10 P.M. from May through September. From October to May, the Skydeck is open from 10 A.M. to 8 P.M. Tickets are $9.95 for adults and $6.95 for children between the ages of 3 and 11. The charge for seniors is $7.95. For more information, visit www.the-skydeck.com or call 312-875-9696.

Largest Catsup Bottle
Collinsville, IL

At 170 feet tall, this bottle could host a lot of barbecues. The water tower was built in 1949. According to the official catsup bottle history, it all started in 1891 with the Collinsville Canning and Packing Company. In 1907, Everett and Elgin Brooks took over and started operating first under the name of Triumph Catsup and Pickle Company, and then Brooks Tomato Products Company.

The company changed ownership a couple more times and in 1933, G.S.

Suppiger Company was the owner. But the Brooks name had gained quite a reputation, so the name stayed the same. The plant produced tasty catsup, chili beans, soups, and sauces. Giant signs went up in St. Louis and in Belleville. In 1949, the giant catsup bottle was born. The structure was built to hold 100,000 gallons of water, some of which was used at the catsup factory, but most was for fire protection. Like many superlatives, this giant generated publicity for its company. The Suppigers sold their share of the company in 1960 and the catsup operations were moved to Indiana, to the dismay of local catsup lovers in town.

The factory was turned into a warehouse; and in 1993, the property went up for sale, creating an uncertain future for the catsup bottle. A catsup bottle preservation group was formed. The owner was willing to deed the property to the city, but Collinsville's rulers were worried about the cost of the repairs. The preservation group sprung into action and started fund-raising. Volunteers spent two years raising $80,000 to repaint and restore the tower. It was fully restored in 1995. The restoration aimed to revive the bottle and downtown Collinsville, a town of 22,000 not far from St. Louis, on the Illinois side. The area still hosts a World's Largest Catsup Bottle Summerfest, with a car show and family-friendly fun.

Today you can get souvenirs (postcards, t-shirts, and even a Catsup Bottle Coloring and Activity Fun Book) at Ashmann's Pharmacy and Gifts downtown at 209 E. Main.

➥ **Directions:** From I-70, exit at 159 southbound. The catsup bottle is 3.5 miles from the freeway, at 800 S. Morrison Ave. (aka Illinois Route 159.) For more information, visit www.catsupbottle.com or call 618-345-5598.

INDIANA

Giant Egg
Mentone, IN

The egg capital of the country deserves to have an egg in the middle of town. Mentone calls itself the egg basket of the Midwest, and even holds an egg festival in June to prove it. The egg was built in the 1940s, but it has contenders for the largest, especially in Washington State.

Author photo

➤ **Directions:** The egg is on the main drag through town: Highway 25, also known as Main Street. The egg is on the corner of Main and Morgan.

Largest Stuffed Steer
Kokomo, IN

The striking difference between Old Ben and some of the other livestock featured among Midwest superlatives is that Ben once lived. This is no painted bull or fiberglass Holstein. Ben was once flesh and blood. Today he is just pelt. But when he was alive, he was a thing of wonder. When he was born in nearby Miami County on the farm of Mike and John Murphy, he was called the world's largest calf, weighing in at 135 pounds. A century later, people are still in awe of him.

Ben's daddy was a Hereford bull and his mom was a long rangy grade shorthorn. People came to see him because of his size—he was 4,720 pounds at his last weighing. When Ben was exhibited in the state fair, the Murphy brothers were offered money from circuses who wanted his moxie in their show. But the brothers kept him on the farm, a few miles north of Kokomo, where he lived to be eight years old. In 1910 he fell on ice and broke a leg. A farmer was called in to shoot him.

His hide was stuffed and mounted, which is what we see today. He stayed a part of the Murphy farm post-mortem until the Murphy's sold it in 1919 and gave him to the city. He has been in Highland Park ever since.

The rest of him? Ben probably lives on in the people around Kokomo. Legend has it that his final "culinary destination" was a frankfurter shop in Indianapolis—probably one that sold jumbo dogs!

No one is sure why Ben was so big.

➤ **Directions:** Ben is housed in a stone and glass home in Highland Park. From Highway 31, exit at Indiana 22/Markland Avenue and head west. At Washington Street, turn south. Go west at Defenbaugh Street, which will go into the park. Look for Old Ben Drive, where Ben lives. For more information, visit www.kokomo-in.org or call the visitor's bureau at 800-837-0971.

Largest Stump
Kokomo, IN

The sycamore stump is called one of the original Howard County landmarks. The tree originally stood at the west end of the county, about two miles north of New London along the banks of Wildcat Creek. They say the tree was 100 feet tall and 800 years old when a storm broke it down to a hollow stump. Soon after, the stump was moved to Highland Park, where it still remains. You can see decades old initials carved into the stump.

➡ **Directions:** See directions for Ben, the largest stuffed steer. Like Ben, the stump is in a window-lined building, so you can't touch it, but you can look in at it.

Biggest Ball of Paint
Alexandria, IN

What started as a baseball has steadily grown to a 1,300 pound giant. Mike Carmichael and his wife, Glenda, have been painting the same baseball for 27 years. During this time, they've applied more than 18,000 coats of paint. A pictorial on their website shows who has been involved—from their son, when he was three years old back in the 1970s, to special visitors.

Carmichael explains on his website that he got his start in ball painting as a high school baseball player. He was working a summer job at a paint store when he and a friend started playing catch and whoops, the baseball ended up covered in paint. They cleaned up the paint but left the baseball in its artistic state. Carmichael painted it through the remainder of his high school years and kept track of the number of coats. He quit after 1,000 coats and donated the ball to the alumni museum. A few years later he started on a new baseball that was 9 inches in circumference when it began. Now it is so big, Carmichael had to build it its own room.

➡ **Directions:** The Ball of Paint is located on 200 West between State Route 128 and State Route 28. In 2004, Carmichael was working on building a barn so that the ball of paint can entertain its own visitors. Donations accepted toward the construction fund. For more information, visit http://ballofpaint.freehosting.net.

IOWA

Biggest Bull
Audubon, IA

Weighing in at 45 tons, Albert the Bull could put on quite a barbeque, except that he is made of steel and 65 gallons of paint. He was born in 1964 in honor of Operation T-Bone, a beef marketing campaign and a "tribute to the nation's beef industry." He's named after the Audubon banker who started the event. The operation marked the shipment of roughly 50 carloads of beef sent to Chicago markets. Today he stands outside in Albert Park.

Albert was thought up by Donald Olesen, a member of the junior Chamber of Commerce. There were few tourist attractions in western Iowa and locals thought a giant bull just might be enough to steer visitors to Audubon. More than 20,000 people stop to see him ever year.

The city donated the land at the south edge of town for his home. He

Author photo

was designed as a Hereford because it's more colorful than other beef cattle. Most of the labor was done by the Jaycees.

Albert has been featured in the movie *Beethoven's 3rd* and was a question on the TV game show *Jeopardy*.

You can hear his history at a kiosk that has an audio history of Albert talking about his past. Photos of his construction mark his creation. It took two years to build him and 65 gallons of paint to cover him.

➡ **Directions:** From northbound highway 71, Albert is on the east side of the road in Albert Park. Watch for the Albert City Park sign. Take a right into Albert Park, where Albert is always available for visitors. For more information, contact the Audubon Chamber of Commerce at 712-563-2742.

Biggest Swedish Coffee Pot and Cup
Stanton, IA

Valkommen! You have entered the land of the Vikings. Warning: if you are not into interesting designs painted on water towers, do not visit this site. You could probably write a book on all the water tower designs out there in the world, but we'll save that for someone else and just say here that this is a reflection of the Swedish heritage in the area. In the middle of town is a Swedish Cultural Center. (Signs around town will direct you there.) A statue of two immigrants represents the 1.3 million Swedes who came to America in the early part of the 1900s. For those old enough to remember the commercials, the town is also the birthplace of Virginia Christine, who was Mrs. Olsen in the Folgers Coffee advertisements.

➡ **Directions:** To see the water tower, enter Stanton from Highway 34 and stay left over the bridge to get on Halland Avenue. Watch the horizon! The Center is located at 410 Hilltop Avenue and is open Tuesday through Saturday from 1 to 4 P.M. and possibly other times at the request of visitors. For more information, call 712-829-2840.

Largest Popcorn Ball
Sac City, IA

The popcorn ball has a fabled history in Sac County. Town residents built a six-foot, 2,225-pound popcorn ball in 1995. Ah, but those meddling kids! Not long after the Sac Ball was created, a group of Wisconsin Boy

Scouts built a bigger ball—2,377 pounds. Sac City blew up their ball and moved on until 2004 when they made their next creation.

The new ball is 3,100 pounds of popcorn and syrup. Nearly 50 people spent more than eight hours building it at Noble Popcorn Farms. "We wanted to highlight the popcorn industry in Sac County," said Shirley Phillips, who works for the county's tourism and economic development section.

The plant manager at Noble Popcorn, where the beast was built, reported that it took 910 pounds of popcorn, 1500 pounds of sugar and 690 pounds of syrup. Temporary "World's Largest Popcorn Ball" tattoos were made for the occasion and put up for sale at the Sac City chamber of commerce. At seven feet tall, the Iowans think their popcorn ball is once again the biggest in the land. There are no plans to blow up this one.

➡ **Directions:** The popcorn ball is located at the Sac City Museum on U.S. Highway 20, on the corner of 13th and Main Street in Sac City. A window allows passersby to see it without going into the museum. For more information, visit www.saccountyiowa.com or call 712-662-7383.

Giant Strawberry
Strawberry Point, IA

The statue, built in 1967, is 15 feet high and 12 feet wide. Dimples and all, it stands 29 feet off the ground above city hall. It is 1,430 pounds and a force to be reckoned with. After the original strawberry was installed, a huge wind storm toppled it. It crashed down in front of city hall on State Highway 3 and 13, blocking the road. No one was injured. The new strawberry was installed the same year with a more secure anchoring system.

The town was originally called Franklin, but someone realized another Franklin had already been established in Iowa. Settlers in the area were impressed by the abundance of wild strawberries and the town became known as Strawberry Point. Now a giant red strawberry guards the city hall downtown.

➡ **Directions:** The strawberry is located at City Hall, 111 Commercial Street, near the intersection of Highways 3 and 13. For more information, visit www.strawberrypt.com or call 563-933-4400.

KANSAS

Largest Ball of Twine
Cawker City, KS

"Sure is huge!" wrote one man who visited from Virginia. The largest ball of twine sits under a canopy in downtown Cawker City on a slab of concrete, and flocked by signs pointing out its greatness. There is a mailbox containing a register where visitors can sign their names and write a comment. You can see how far people have come to see this giant beige ball. (New York, California . . . it is a long list.) Even the town signs welcome you to the home of the world's largest ball of twine. And that's not all! Paint signs on the sidewalk direct you to a twine walk. Follow the paint and you'll walk past paintings incorporating the twine ball. There's a rendition of Van Gogh's "Starry Starry Night", with twine ball; a Salvador Dali, with twine ball; and even Egyptian and American patriotic themed paintings, with twine balls.

The town holds a "twine-a-thon" every year during the third weekend

Author photo

in August. The last entry, from Aug. 15, 2003, cataloged the ball at 17,670 pounds.

Frank Stoeber began the ball on his farm in 1953 using twine from bales of hay. It was 5,000 pounds by 1957. He passed away in 1974, but the city still honors him with the twine-a-thon and the recognition that he began something great for the town.

The Great Plains Gallery, across the street, has souvenirs and Basco's Market on the same street has postcards and information. Founded in 1870, legend has it that the city was named by four founders who decided that the winner of a poker game would name it. E.H. Cawker won. Today Cawker City is a small town with about 500 people.

➤ **Directions:** The ball of twine is outside under a canopy and is always open to the public. It is located on Highway 24 (Wisconsin Street) on the south side of the Highway in town, a half-block west of Lake Drive. For more information, visit www.skyways.org/towns/cawker or call 785-781-4713.

Biggest Hand Dug Well
Greensburg, KS

Initially, it might seem strange to want to see a hole in the ground. But ask around, and you'll find that the largest hand-dug well is a well-known attraction in the Sunflower State. Millions of people have come to visit the Big Well, which is 109 feet deep and 32 feet in diameter. The well was completed in 1888 to serve thirsty people of the plains. Railroads were being built across Kansas and water was needed to serve the steam locomotives, as well as the growing population.

According to the local historians, it took the combined efforts of local farmers, cowboys, and laborers to dig it. They were paid 50 cents to $1 a day for their grueling efforts digging foot after foot with shovels and picks. They lived in tents while working. Stone from the Medicine River, 12 miles away, was used for casing the well. The dirt that was removed was used to level the roads to the quarry.

The well served as the city water supply until 1932. Soon after it was retired, it became the tourist attraction it remains today. Expanding on the wishing well idea, visitors have tossed everything from shoes to rubber snakes into the well; the town cleaned out the bottom of the well in 1990. The findings are on display at the gift shop. Visitors can walk 105 steps to the bottom, which is lit up.

➡ **Directions:** Greensburg is located on U.S. Highway 54 in south central Kansas, east of the Highway 183 junction. The well is located at 315 S. Sycamore. From Highway 54, turn south on Sycamore and drive three blocks. The Big Well is open from 8 A.M. to 8 P.M. everyday between Memorial Day and Labor Day. Hours are fewer during winter months. Admission is $1.50 for adults and $1.25 for children between the ages of four and 13. For more information, visit www.bigwell.org or call 800-207-7369.

Biggest Concrete Outdoor Free Swimming Pool
Garden City, KS

Long billed as the biggest, concrete, outdoor free swimming pool, the folks at Garden City had to take out one word of their creation—free. It now costs a dollar to get into the big concrete outdoor swimming pool, which is 220 feet by 330 feet. When the entire pool is open, there are 17 lifeguards on duty. If you're five years old or younger you can get in for free. So in a sense, it's still free. (But if you're five years old and you can read this, you're ahead of yourself and should flip to the Massachusetts section for information on college). According to the city, the hand-dug pool was built in 1922 and it was so big, they put a boat in it for a promotional photo.

➡ **Directions:** The Garden City Regional Pool is located in Finnup Park at 403 S. 4th Street, which is also where the zoo is located. From U.S. 83, take the bypass and head east. Take the 3rd Street exit, which will turn into 4th Street. The pool is open from 1 P.M. to 6 P.M. Monday through Thursday and from 1 P.M. to 7 P.M. on weekends and holidays, provided the outside temperature is 70 degrees or warmer. For more information, visit www.garden-city.org/pool.html.

Biggest Painting and Easel
Goodland, KS

This gigantic easel stands 80 feet tall near the Kansas/Colorado border. It is one in a series of easels meant to encourage art by helping local, national, and international artists paint giant works of art on canvases that are 24 by 32 feet large.

The series is called the Van Gogh Project and its ultimate goal is to erect hand-painted reproductions of Van Gogh's seven sunflower paintings. It was started by Cameron Cross, a Canadian artist and teacher who helped build the first giant easel in Altona, Canada in 1998. The second is in Emerald, Australia. The Kansas easel is the third in the series.

Kansas has one (along with cities in Canada and Australia) because it has a connection to sunflowers. (It is officially the "sunflower state" and if you travel at the right time, you can see them dotting the landscape.)

➤ **Directions:** From Interstate 70, take exit 19 and go north on Highway 24. Take a right on Cherry Street and you will see the easel on the right. It's lit up at night and a park is planned for the site. For more information, visit www.thebigeasel.com or call 785-899-7130.

KENTUCKY

Longest Cave
Mammoth Cave National Park, KY

This cave system is the longest recorded in the world, with more than 360 miles of caves. There are hundreds more caves within the park that are disconnected from the major system. The National Park Service describes this area as an integrated set of drainage basins that covers more than 400 square miles. More than 300 million years ago, an ancient sea covered the United States and laid the foundation of the cave system—limestone. An ancient river deposited sandstone and shale cap. Both the sea and river disappeared, and over time erosion started working away at shale cap and limestone. Rain formed streams which hollowed out the caves. Inside the caves, there are geological features that have developed over thousands of years: stalagmites, stalactites, and gypsum formations.

The environment inside is very sensitive, and the park system has had to work carefully to try and balance the needs of the cave with the visiting population. The natural, yet alien-looking features are described with names like Snowball Room, Grand Central Station, Frozen Niagara, Bottomless Pit, and Bridal Altar. Currently, there are 13 cave tours offered. Some are geared toward parents with little kids, while the Wild Cave tour is geared toward the more adventuresome. The Wild Cave tour is more than six hours long, limited to 14 people, costs $46, and includes crawls through areas that are nine inches high. (Helmets, lights and kneepads are provided, but bring your own boots.)

➡ **Directions:** Mammoth Cave National Park is accessible from Kentucky Highways 70 and 255. The park is open year round. Tours vary by season and usually require a fee. For more information, visit www.nps.gov/maca or call 270-758-2180.

Largest Baseball Bat
Louisville, KY

This bat is so big, we're not sure even the giant Viking of Alexandria, Minnesota could swing it. The world's biggest bat is made of steel, weighs 68,000 pounds, and stands 120 feet tall outside the Louisville Slugger Museum. The bat is an exact scale replica of Babe Ruth's Louisville Slugger. It's signed by Bud Hillerich as a tribute to the man who turned the company's first bat.

➡ **Directions:** The bat is outside of the museum, which is located at 800 W. Main Street in Louisville, on the corner of Main and 8th streets. From I-64, exit on 3rd Street. Take a right on River Road and a left on 8th Street. For more information, visit www.sluggermuseum.com or call 502-588-7228.

Credit: Kentucky Department of Travel

LOUISIANA

Longest Bridge
Second Lake Pontchartrain Causeway, LA

This 24.2 mile bridge connects Mandeville and New Orleans. The lake was named for the Count de Pontchartrain who was minister of finance for Louis XIV, the king of France for whom Louisiana was named. The twin spans parallel each other, each heading one direction. Periodic cross-overs allow turnarounds. The spans were constructed with more than 9,000 concrete pilings. Engineers used barges to carry pieces of the bridge out to construction points in the lake. The first span opened in 1956 as a two-way, two lane bridge. A second span opened in 1969 and thereafter, each span goes one-way. Every weekday, more than 30,000 cars cross the bridge. The causeway also serves as an official hurricane evacuation route for the city of New Orleans.

Technically, Lake Pontchartrain is an estuary because it has salt water content. It is the largest inland estuary in the United States.

➤ **Directions:** You can get on the causeway in New Orleans from Interstate 610 or from U.S. Highway 61. The toll is $3, but only in one direction. For more information, visit www.thecauseway.com.

Biggest Domed Stadium
New Orleans, LA

Somewhere between a spaceship and a giant eyeball is the Louisiana Superdome—the largest enclosed stadium in the world. The area of the roof alone is 9.7 acres and the diameter of the dome is 680 feet. The stadium, home of the New Orleans Saints and the Sugar Bowl, opened in 1975. Since then, it has served the masses who have come to see everyone from the Rolling Stones to the Pope.

➤ **Directions:** There are no tours. The Superdome is located in central New Orleans on Sugar Bowl Drive. From westbound Interstate 10, take the Orleans Avenue exit. Turn left on Orleans, which becomes Loyola Avenue. Turn right on Girod Street. For more information, visit www.superdome.com or call 504-587-3663.

Largest Steamboat
New Orleans, LA

The "American Queen" is a $65 million steamboat launched in 1995 by the Delta Queen Steamboat Company. It is the biggest steamboat ever made and carries passengers through the rivers of the south and beyond. The ship is 418 feet long and is propelled by one paddlewheel that weighs 45 tons. It has six passenger decks and a Grand Saloon modeled after opera houses from the 1800s. The Ladies Parlor has Victorian antiques and the Gentleman's card room has a television hidden behind a boar's head. (Ladies are allowed in the men's room.) The American Queen is propelled by vintage steam engines that were salvaged from a ship previously owned by the U.S. Army Corps of Engineers.

➡ **Directions:** The steamboat travels along the Mississippi, so you might spot it there or in ports of call in New Orleans, Baton Rouge, St. Francisville, or in Natchez, Mississippi. In New Orleans, the steamboat docks at the Robin Street Wharf, behind the downtown convention center. For more information, visit www.deltaqueen.com or call 800-543-1949.

MAINE

Largest Rotating Globe
Yarmouth, ME

The earth's largest globe was made by a map maker, DeLorme, in 1998. Eartha is her name and she's housed in a three-story glass atrium in the company's headquarters. Just like our real Earth, Eartha tilts at 23.5 degrees and she rotates. She weighs nearly 6,000 pounds and took two years to build. Her skin, so they say, is 792 map sections made using satellite imagery; this is how Earth looks from space. The sphere of the globe has a diameter of 41 feet. Every aspect was developed using computer technology, including mapping the data, which took a year to compile. The company built a database to make the globe reflect vegetation, ocean depths, road networks, and

Credit: DeLorme

cities. Its scale is 1:1,000,000; every inch on the globe equals nearly 16 miles. The globe's interior is made of aluminum tubing in place of hot magma.

➤ **Directions:** The DeLorme Map Store and lobby with Eartha are open seven days a week from 9:30 A.M. to 6 P.M. There is no fee to see Eartha. From Interstate 295, take exit 17. Take a right off the ramp and the building is immediately on the right. For more information, visit www.delorme.com or call 800-642-0970.

Largest Whirlpool
Off the coast of Maine, near Eastport, ME

This whirlpool called the Old Sow, is in the Atlantic Ocean between Eastport Maine (the easternmost city in the U.S.) and Deer Island, New Brunswick. Currents, tides, and flow from the St. Croix River team with underwater trenches and mountains to help form the whirlpool. It's called the largest whirlpool in the Western Hemisphere.

There's even an Old Sow Whirlpool Survivors' Association, where you can get an Old Sow Whirlpool Survivor Certificate, suitable for framing, according to members.

➤ **Directions:** The Deer Island Ferry goes near the whirlpool, or you can look for it from the north end of Water Street in Eastport. For more information, visit www.oldsowwhirlpool.com.

Largest Chocolate Moose
Scarborough, ME

The folks at Len Libby Chocolate wanted to give new meaning to the words "chocolate mousse." So they created Lenny, a 1,700 pound moose—antlers and all—made of chocolate. He is life-sized like the kind you might find in the woods around Maine. You can visit Lenny in his natural habitat, in the store amongst a forest of caramels, nut clusters, peanut brittle, fudge, taffy, and even chocolate lobster pops. There's also a video about how he was created.

Len Libby Handmade Candies opened for business in 1926. In 1949, the business was sold to Fernand Hemond, who still runs the business today with his family.

➤ **Directions:** Len Libby is located at 419 U.S. Route One. From U.S. 95, take exit 6. Head south on Route 1 to get to the store. For more information, visit www.lenlibby.com or call 207-883-4897.

MARYLAND

Oldest Continually Operating City Market
Baltimore, MD

Even before people needed centralized government, they needed food. The folks at Lexington Market pride themselves on being nearly as old as the United States. The market opened in 1782 on the original site it still occupies today. An American Revolutionary general, John Eager Howard, donated the land for the market on his way home from the war. The market was named after the Battle of Lexington. Soon after, on the open field, the site became home to the bartering and buying of hams, eggs, and produce. As time passed, the market grew. In 1803, a shed was constructed at Eutaw and Lexington streets. Then the market moved to Greene Street. Historic footage of the place shows ladies shopping in frilly hats and gloves. Men wore ties.

The market was revitalized in 2002 and now is home to 140 merchants selling everything from fresh meat to donuts, produce, newspapers, and specialty foods that can be eaten on the spot or cooked at home.

➡ **Directions:** The market is located at 400 W. Lexington Street. From U.S. 40 eastbound, turn right on Greene Street and turn left on Lexington. For more information, visit www.lexingtonmarket.com or call 410-685-6169.

Oldest Continuously Operating State House
Annapolis, MD

History is thick inside the Maryland State House. From 1783 until 1784, the Old Senate Chamber was the home of the Continental Congress. On the floor is a plaque marking the place where George Washington stood and resigned his position as commander in chief of the Continental Army in 1783. A month after the event, the Treaty of Paris was signed here, officially ending the Revolutionary War.

The statehouse was built between 1772 and 1779. It is the only statehouse to have served as the nation's capitol. The building has grown with age. A Colonial Revival section was added to the building between 1902 and 1905. A black line across the floor marks where the old building ended and the new building began.

Inside the statehouse you can find pieces of the moon brought back from Apollo 11. The building also contains the 1859 original painting "Washington Resigning His Commission" painted by Edwin White.

As a bonus, the top of the State House claims the largest all-wooden dome in the United States. Even the nails are made of wood.

The Senate and House of Delegates chambers are open to the public. Inside you can see the electronic voting boards and desk switches used by members for their votes.

Directions: The State House is located at 91 State Circle. From State Highway 70 eastbound, turn left on College Avenue/MD 450. Turn right on North St. and enter the State Circle roundabout. Tours are available. The visitor's center is open everyday but Dec. 25. Hours are 9 A.M. to 5 P.M. Monday through Friday and 10 A.M. to 4 P.M. Saturday and Sunday. For more information, call www.mdwelcome.com or call 410-974-3400.

Oldest Continuously Operating Airport
College Park Airport, MD

A runway, a couple planes . . . is this really that interesting? Possibly not until you consider all the firsts that occurred here. The first scheduled U.S. postal service flight took off from here, serving New York and Philadelphia. The first Army aviation school was held here. According to the museum, the airport was founded in 1909 for the Wright Brothers' instruction of military aviators. It has added much to its history since.

Directions: The museum is located at 1985 Corporal Frank Scott Drive. From I-495, take exit 23, to Kenilworth Avenue. Turn south on Kenilworth (Rte. 201) and turn right at Corporal Frank Scott Drive. The museum is open daily from 10 A.M. to 5 P.M. except on major holidays. Admission is $4 for adults and $2 for children and students. For more information, visit www.collegeparkaviationmuseum.com or call 301-864-6029.

MASSACHUSETTS

Oldest Baseball Stadium
Boston, MA

Fenway Park is the second home of the Red Sox, which started in 1901 as the Boston Pilgrims and played at the Huntington Avenue Grounds, now part of the Northeastern University campus, according to Sox history.

Author photo

The first professional game at Fenway, named after its location in the Fenway section of Boston, was played on April 20, 1912. The stadium was built to fit between existing city streets. Lights were added in 1947. The park has one of the last hand-operated score boards in the Major League.

If you happen to be in Boston during the Red Sox off season, you can still visit Fenway Park on a tour. And even die-hard baseball fans have found satisfaction in this tour despite the lack of a ball game, hotdogs, or beer. On this tour, you can visit the press box, the 406 Club, and seats that some of us will never be able to afford. You can get the story behind the Green Monster and see the Boston skyline from the upper reaches of the park.

➤ **Directions:** Fenway Park is located at 4 Yawkey Way in Boston. On the Boston subway, take the green line to the Kenmore stop. From I-90, the Massachusetts Turnpike, exit at Cambridge, turn right on Storrow Drive East. Take the Fenway exit off Storrow and turn right onto Boylston Street. For more information, visit www.redsox.com or call 617-267-9440.

Oldest Restaurant
Boston, MA

Something about the landing of the pilgrims in Massachusetts has led the state to a lot of "oldest" superlatives. The Union Oyster House is one of them.

Established in 1826, the Union Oyster House is the oldest restaurant with continuous service in the U.S. The building itself is so old, the proprietors say, there are no records of who built it or when. You can see some of the history in the Heritage Room on the second floor. The restaurant is right off the Freedom Trail in Boston and a great place to take a break from the other early American sites in the area. The building where it is located is an old brick building that has been in the same spot for 250 years, before many American states were even part of the union.

The site has plenty of other stories. It once housed a fancy dress goods business, a newspaper called the *Massachusetts Spy*, and a pay station for federal troops serving in the late 1700s. Back when it was a dress goods shop, the Boston waterfront came up to the building. During the Revolution, it's said, the wives of Adams, Hancock, and Quincy sewed bandages on the first floor.

In 1796, the future king of France, Louis Phillippe, lived on the second floor while he was in exile from France. It was a dry goods store until 1826 when it went to the oyster business, with a semi-circular oyster bar, where Daniel Webster was a customer. (He drank brandy and water and ate many plates of oysters.) More modern politicians, including John F. Kennedy, dined here; there is a booth dedicated to JFK upstairs. The building was designated a National Historic Landmark in 2003, but you can still get a dozen kinds of oysters here: a half dozen for around $9. For those who don't partake, there are steaks, salads, and of course, Boston baked beans.

➡ **Directions:** The Union Oyster House is located at 31 Union Street in Boston on the Freedom Trail near Faneuil Hall. From Interstate 93 southbound, take exit 24/Callahan Tunnel. At the bottom of the exit ramp, turn right onto North Street. Go past the Bostonian Hotel and take a right at the corner on Union Street. The restaurant will be on the right. You can also take the subway. Take the blue or green lines to Government Center or the Orange Line to Haymarket. The restaurant is open from 11 A.M. to 9:30 P.M. from Sunday through Thursday and from 11 A.M. to 10 P.M. on Friday and Saturday. For more information, visit www.unionoysterhouse.com or call 617-227-2750.

Oldest Tavern
Boston, MA

The windows are open. Tourists are milling past. And you're sitting in the Bell-in-Hand enjoying a tall, cool ale in a pub that is older than your great-great-great grandparents. The Bell-in-Hand was first owned by Jimmy Wilson, the town crier for 50 years. He reported on the Boston Tea Party and American Independence. And when he retired, he opened a tavern, naming it after his signature signal: his bell.

The bar is airy and has been brought into the modern world with televisions and live music performed on the weekends. But it still has its original charm. No hard liquor was sold at the Bell, only ale. They say Wilson sold it in two mugs: one for the ale and the second for the froth. Tavern favorites include clam chowder, burgers and sandwiches.

➤ **Directions:** The Bell-in-Hand is located at 45 Union Street and neighbors the Union Oyster House. Bell-in-Hand is open from 11:30 A.M. to 2 A.M. Monday through Friday and from noon to 2 A.M. on Saturday and Sunday. See the Oyster House directions for more information on how to get there or call 617-227-2098.

Oldest College
Boston, MA

Harvard College is the oldest institution of higher education in the country, founded in 1636, just 16 years after the Pilgrims landed in Plymouth, not too far from here. The college started with nine students and one teacher. It is named for John Harvard of Charlestown, a minister who left his library and half his estate to Harvard in 1638. According to the school's history, many of the early graduates became ministers in Puritan congregations. In the early 1700s, the election of a president who wasn't a clergyman helped steer the college away from Puritanism and toward intellectual independence.

➤ **Directions:** The subway goes to Harvard. Take the red line toward Alewife to the Harvard Square. Once there, you can take a free, one-hour historical tour of the campus. For more information, visit www.harvard.edu or call 617-495-1573.

MICHIGAN

Largest Stove
Detroit, MI

According to the state, back in the 1800s, Detroit was once considered the "Stove Capital of the World." The Michigan Stove Company wanted to make an exhibit for the 1893 Columbian Exposition in Chicago, so it built a giant stove. Sculptors carved the stove in oak and painted it to look like metal. It measures 25 feet tall and weighs 15 tons. At the exhibit it stood on a platform 20 feet tall over an exhibit of real stoves. After the event, the giant stove was displayed at the factory at Adair and East Jefferson in Detroit.

The stove moved after a company merger but stayed in Detroit. In 1957, Schaefer Bakeries leased the stove to advertise their bread. Years of Michigan winters took their toll and in 1974, the stove was dismantled and placed into storage. In 1998, the Michigan State Fair management decided to organize local leaders to get the stove back out in the public eye. They succeeded and today the stove has been restored and is on display at the Michigan State Fairgrounds—more than 100 years after it attracted people to Michigan stoves at the Columbian Exposition.

➤ **Directions:** The stove is located inside the Michigan State Fairgrounds on Spartan Street, between Kiddie Land and Hudson Auditorium, near the parking lots off Woodward Avenue. It is on a knoll. The fairgrounds are located at the corner of Eight Mile Rd. and Woodward Avenue, two miles west of Interstate 75. The fairgrounds are open year round, typically from 8 A.M. to 5 P.M. There may be an admission charge to enter the fairgrounds if an event is occurring. For more information, visit www.michigan.gov or call 313-369-8250.

Biggest Tire
Allen Park, MI

Where else but the Motor City would you expect to find an 80 foot tall tire? The tire was first created as a Ferris Wheel for the 1964–1965 New York World's Fair. When the fair ended, the tire was shipped by rail in 188 sections to Detroit. After the fair, Uniroyal tire set it up at its Allen Park, Michigan sales office. According to the folks at Uniroyal, more than two million people rode the tire at the fair, including Jacqueline Kennedy and her children. Each ride cost 25 cents. The tire has been renovated several times over the years including in 1998 when a giant nail was placed in the tread to demonstrate the rubber's durability. It would take 960 Uniroyal passenger tires to make the Uniroyal Giant.

➤ **Directions:** The giant tire is located off Interstate 94 in Allen Park near the airport. For more information, visit www.uniroyal.com/about/gianttire.html or call 877-UNIROYAL.

Largest Living Roof
Dearborn, MI

Calm, green grass is typically the last thing you think of when you're talking trucks. Ford Motor Company has been working to change that with earth-friendly projects like the living roof it installed on the top of its Dearborn Truck Plant. In 2003, the company installed a 10.4 acre "living roof" on the roof of the final assembly building—the biggest living roof project in the world. The roof has a drought-resistant, perennial ground cover called sedum which absorbs rain and snow and ultimately reduced the amount of run off into nearby streams and rivers. The cover protects the roof from solar radiation and storms, making the builders think this roof could last twice as long as a conventional roof. The sedum plants grow less than six inches tall, so no one's going to have to worry about mowing the roof.

➤ **Directions:** Ford had tours of its Rouge Factory from 1924 until 1980, and stopped offering them until 2004. You can see the living roof from an 80-foot high observation deck at the visitor's center on the Rouge Factory Tour. Tours leave from the Henry Ford Museum daily every half hour from 9:30 A.M. to 2:30 P.M. The museum is located at 20900 Oakwood Boulevard in Dearborn. From Interstate 94, take the Southfield Freeway (Michigan 39) north to Oakwood Boulevard. Go left on Oakwood for 2 miles until you reach the factory. Touring the Rouge costs $14 for adults and $10 for children. The museum is closed on Thanksgiving and December 25. For more information, visit www.thehenryford.org or call 313-982-6100.

Biggest Padlock
Escanaba, MI

Computer aided design students at Bay de Noc Community College, in the northern reaches of Michigan, have the opportunity to take a team problem-solving class. During the semester long class, students can choose to design and build a project that breaks a world record. In 1998, students wanted to build the world's biggest tricycle, and they did. The trike, which cost $6,000 to build, functions if two people ride it. Students rode it 100 feet to prove that it worked. This entry was going to be about that tricycle until we learned that the tricycle (gasp) has been disassembled. It's in pieces on campus if you want to stop by and pay your respects. The night before the class officially measured the 23-foot tricycle, a wind storm blew it over. No one was hurt, except for a car that lost a mirror and the trike did sustain some damage. The National Guard brought out a crane to set it upright. It had to be repainted and was still wet when the inaugural ride took place. Another class built a cardboard boat for 14 people.

The giant padlock failed to get into the record books because someone in Cyprus or someplace built a bigger one. But this book is about superlatives in the USA and this is the biggest padlock in our country. Although not as fun for small children to play with, a padlock has its merits.

Instructor Jerry Havill said the problem-solving class teaches students to work as a team and manage long-term projects. Students raised money and spent $15,000 to build the 2,800 pound padlock. It is located on campus near the M-TEC building and was built complete with a functioning key.

► **Directions:** Bay de Noc Community College is located in Escanaba, on the eastern side of Michigan's Upper Peninsula on Lake Michigan near the Wisconsin border. The college is located at 2001 N. Lincoln. The padlock is located outside and is technically always open to the public. For more information, visit www.baydenoc.cc.mi.us/ or call 906-786-5802.

Longest Porch
Mackinac Island, MI

Mackinac Island is small and no cars are allowed on the island. Transportation is by bike or on foot. The only way to get here is by boat or plane. The main hotel, the Grand Hotel is very large and it has a porch that could hold all the residents of the Upper Peninsula. It is 660 feet long. The Grand Hotel opened in 1887 for vacationers from Chicago, Detroit and other Midwestern and Canadian cities. Rooms were $3 when the hotel opened. Now it costs triple that just to see the porch if you're not a guest. They say in the 1890s, the hotel porch became the meeting place for all of the islanders. The history continued with presidential visits, a speech by Mark Twain, and finally an automobile ban that was eventually enforced in the 1930s. Movies have been filmed here, including *This Time for Keeps* and *Somewhere in Time.*

➡ **Directions:** Mackinac Island is in between the upper and lower peninsulas of Michigan. Ferries to Mackinac Island are available in Mackinaw City (on the lower peninsula) or St. Ignace (on the upper peninsula.) There's a $10 fee to check out the hotel and porch if you're not staying at the hotel. For more information, visit www.grandhotel.com or call 800-33–GRAND.

Largest College Football Stadium Capacity
Ann Arbor, MI

The number of people who can watch the University of Michigan Wolverines play in this stadium is almost as large as the number of people who live in the college town of Ann Arbor. A game in The Big House is a day surrounded by 107,500 people, some of them die-hard Wolverine fans. According to UM history, Michigan Stadium was built on land with an underground spring. It was so wet and soggy, it swallowed up a crane that remains under the stadium today. When it opened, it could seat 84,401 and was the largest college-owned stadium. The first game was played in 1927, when the Wolverines beat Ohio Wesleyan. Stadium capacity was increased several times before reaching today's number.

➡ **Directions:** From Interstate 94, exit at #175, and turn right on Ann Arbor-Saline Road. It turns into Main Street. The stadium is on the corner of Main Street and Stadium. For more information, visit www.mgoblue.com or call 734-647-BLUE.

Biggest Chainsaw and Rifle
Ishpeming, MI

In the Upper Peninsula of Michigan, the area is wooded. So it is reasonable to expect that you'd find the biggest chainsaw and the biggest rifle . . . both items that are used in the forest. Both are located at Da Yoopers Tourist Trap and Museum—a store named after the name given to folks who live in the U.P.—da yoopers.

The chainsaw is Big Gus. The rifle is Big Ernie. Both are bigger than cars and both really work. The superlatives are outside the shop and visible from the highway.

➡ **Directions:** Da Yoopers is located on U.S. 41 west of Ishpeming. Hours are 9 A.M. to 6 P.M. Monday through Thursday, 9 A.M. to 8 P.M. on Friday, 9 A.M. to 6 P.M. on Saturday, and 10 A.M. to 6 P.M. on Sunday. For more information, visit www.dayoopers.com or call 800-628-9978.

Largest Weathervane
Montague, MI

A giant schooner looks out over White Lake on the largest weathervane. The silver and black tower is 48 feet tall and 14 feet long. It was hand forged in aluminum by Whitehall Products, a local company that builds weathervanes and signs. The company built its biggest in 1984 and donated the 4,300 pound finished product to the town. It is an operating weathervane with a weather station at its base.

➡ **Directions:** Montague is about 16 miles north of Muskegon. From U.S. Highway 31, take the business route to town. The weathervane stands outside at the corner of Dowling and Water streets in downtown Montague. For more information, visit www.whitelake.org or call 800-879-9702.

Biggest Mosque
Dearborn, MI

The Islamic Center of America has more than 3,000 members in its congregation and has been serving the Muslim population in the Detroit area since 1963. In 2004, the center put the finishing touches on a new mosque that was expected to be the largest in America. The new mosque will have space for 1,000 people. The complex will also hold a museum, library, community center, and school. Its symbolic dome is nearly 40 feet in diameter. The project began in 1999. The Muslim community in the Detroit area is the biggest concentration of Muslims outside of the Middle East. For a tour, call ahead.

➡ **Directions:** The new mosque is located at 19500 Ford Road in Dearborn, east of Greenfield. For more information, visit www.icofa.com or call 313-582-7442.

MINNESOTA

Oldest Rock
Granite Falls, MI

Who knew? Here on the banks of the Minnesota River are some of the oldest exposed rocks ever discovered in the world. Geologists think that the rock here was formed nearly 4 billion years ago.

According to the Minnesota Department of Natural Resources, gneiss is rock formed when granite and other rocks are put under intense heat and pressure within the earth. The rocks were pushed to the earth through volcanic activity millions of years ago.

➤ **Directions:** The rocks are located just next to the Yellow Medicine County Museum, which is on the bank of the Minnesota River at the junction of Highways 212 and 23/67. From Highway 23, turn on to East 67. The museum is open from Thursday to Saturday from 11 A.M. to 5 P.M. and on Sundays from noon to 5 P.M.

Author photo

Biggest Shopping Mall
Bloomington, MN

Located in the suburbs of Minneapolis and St. Paul, there is a shopping experience that could overload even the keenest of consumers—the Mall of America. Traffic lights help to navigate the parking outside, and multilevel parking garages are named after the states. How patriotic! In the mornings, even before the stores open, people walk around the mall for exercise. The shops are all those you would find in any mall, but the difference here is the extras: a water ride and a roller coaster in Camp Snoopy, Legoland, and several Mall of America souvenir stores. There are four levels in the Mall, including a movie theater, numerous restaurants, coffee shops, and of course, shopping.

Directions: The Mall of America is located in Bloomington, at the intersection of Interstate 494 and Highway 77 at 60 East Broadway. Hours for restaurants, attractions, and nightclubs vary. Most stores are open from 10 A.M. to 9:30 P.M. Monday through Friday, 9:30 A.M. to 9:30 P.M. on Saturday, and 11 A.M. to 7 P.M. on Sunday. For more information, visit www.mallofamerica.com or call 800-879-3555.

Credit: Mall of America

Giant Snowman
North St. Paul, MN

Back in the 1970s, North St. Paul's Winter Carnival, with the theme "Snow Frolic", was an event that brought the community together. A giant snowman was built, and people had a good time in the biting Minnesota cold. In the early 1970s, resident Lloyd Koesling and some other local businessmen decided to build a permanent snowman. According to the folks at North St. Paul City Hall, from 1972 to 1974, they constructed the 44-foot tall giant snowman. In 1972, the snowman was adopted as the official city logo. The Frolic went away, but the snowman is still around.

➤ **Directions:** The giant snowman braves the elements on the corner of Highway 36 and Margaret Street in North St. Paul.

Giant Spoon
Minneapolis, MN

Claes Oldenberg and Coosje van Bruggen have dotted the world with giant irregular, yet regular objects. (See Ohio section for directions to their giant rubber stamp.) It all started with a trowel in the Netherlands. Since then they've made more than 40 "Large-Scale Projects" around the world. We don't have all of the American projects in this book, just a few. But there are many more out there dotting our large American landscape, including binoculars in Los Angeles, California, and shuttlecocks (the thing you play badminton with) in Kansas City, Missouri. You can see photos of them on their website. In Minneapolis, they've created a giant spoon and cherry in the Minneapolis Sculpture Garden. It was created in 1988 and is made of stainless steel and aluminum.

➤ **Directions:** The "Spoonbridge and Cherry" sculptures are located in the outdoor sculpture garden next to the Walker Art Museum in downtown Minneapolis. The museum is located on the corner of Vineland Place and Lyndale Avenue South. From Interstate 94, exit at 231B and head north on Lyndale/Hennepin.

Largest Hockey Stick
Eveleth, MN

In the great northlands of the heartland, hockey rules. Eveleth is home to the U.S. Hockey Hall of Fame, the so-called national shrine to American

Author photo

hockey. They say Eveleth is the capital of American hockey, and that no other community the size of Eveleth has produced as many quality players or contributed more to the development of the sport in the U.S. (Nearly 10 percent of the hall's inductees are from Eveleth.) Inside the hall you can read about players, the history and the game for men and women. The hockey stick is a major photo op that shouldn't be missed. Located in downtown Eveleth, the stick rises into the air like a leaning tower of sport.

This is the second stick to grace Eveleth. The first was brought here in 1995 from its birthplace four hours away and required Minnesota State Patrol escort. The site of the stick is "Hockey Plaza" which features white concrete and a face-off circle under a giant puck.

Using the same process used to build standard hockey sticks, Christian Brothers built the 107 foot stick using white and yellow aspens. The shaft was 15 inches thick and 22 inches wide. (Canada built a hockey stick that was longer and heavier, but the Guinness folks turned it down for their book because the sculpture was not considered an authentic hockey stick.)

In 2001, people were concerned with the stick's structural integrity. The stick was removed from its supports and lowered to the ground in 2001.

The city wanted to build a new one, but needed money to do so. The original stick was to be broken into pieces and sold for $5 per piece to raise money for the new endeavor. By 2002 the new stick was on its way to Eveleth from Peshtigo, Wisconsin. Manufactured by Sentinel Structures, the new stick weighs five tons and is 110 feet long.

➡ **Directions:** The hockey stick is located in downtown Eveleth. From Highway 53 Northbound, turn left at the signs for the Hockey Hall of Fame. Follow signs to the "Big Stick." Go left at Hat Trick Ave., then right at Jones. Turn left at Grant. The stick is located outside on the corner of Grant and Monroe. For more information, visit www.evelethchamber.org or call the local chamber of commerce at 218-744-4329.

Largest Open Pit Iron Mine
Hibbing, MN

They call it the Grand Canyon of the Midwest, and when you approach the Hull Rust Mahoning Mine you will see why. The giant hole in the ground is actually the combined efforts of 40 separate mining properties. The landscape has been carved up by more than 100 years of mining, enough that the town of Hibbing actually had to move to get out of the way.

The area's first mining lease was awarded to Frank Hibbing in 1891. The Hull Rust Mine began operating in 1896 and the city followed, too closely. In 1918, all the buildings in the northern side of town were mounted on steel wheels and moved two miles to the south to make room for the mine's expansion. (You can see some old foundations of the old part of town as you drive toward the mine's visiting area.)

The combined Hull Rust Mahoning Mine and Hibbing Taconite open pit covers more than 3,000 acres. The maximum length of the pit from east to west is 3.5 miles.

More than 1.4 billion tons of earth has been removed, which is the equivalent of digging a tunnel from Minnesota to the other side of the earth.

Steel made from the ore from this mine helped make munitions and equipment in both World War I and II. At peak production in the 1940s, one-fourth of the ore mined in the U.S. came from these mines.

There is a parking lot and visitor's center that allows you to get close to the mining operation, which is still pulling up the earth. In the visitor's center, you can look out over the mine and pick up a rust-colored t-shirt or a "Ya You Betcha" magnet.

➡ **Directions:** From highway 169, turn into downtown Hibbing on Howard Street. Go right on Third Avenue and follow signs to Hull Rust, up the hill. Admission is free. The visitor's center is open mid-May through September, Monday through Saturday from 9 A.M. to 5 P.M. and on Sundays from 1 P.M. to 5 P.M. For more information, visit www.irontrail.org or call 218-262-4166.

Biggest Viking
Alexandria, MN

Big Ole is another superlative from the World's Fair Days in the mid 1960s. (His name is pronounced "Oh-lee," not like the Spanish bullfighting "Oh-lay," I learned from the friendly ladies who made me an ice cream cone at the local ice cream store.) The giant Viking was part of Minnesota's display at the New York World's Fair in 1965. He's 28 feet tall and weighs four tons. They say more than 250,000 people went to see him at the World's Fair. (If only we could have seen him riding Wisconsin's talking cow while they were there.)

Author photo

In late 1965, the Viking came home to Alexandria. He's had some tough times. His clothes caught fire, and he had to be moved when a traffic signal went up near his home. In 1991 he got a paint job/makeover and his beard changed from grey to blonde. Storms took their toll and in 1996, Ole was renovated. During that time, while he was under the knife at the Runestone Museum, the roof collapsed on his foot, causing internal damage on his right side.

Ole fans from all over town sent in $27,000 in donations to get him back on his feet. His recovery was celebrated with the Ole Oppe Fest on Memorial Day weekend of 1997. (Oppe means up in Norwegian.) The celebration was so successful, it became an annual event.

Big Ole has some stories behind him. When he sailed from Norway to Minnesota, he left behind a wife named Lena who he met on the way in Greenland. He's known as the first settler in Minnesota. The Runestone Museum in town has detailed history of Scandinavian settlers in the area.

➨ **Directions:** Ole stands outside at Broadway and 2nd Avenue. From Interstate 94, exit at Broadway. Head east for roughly three miles until you come to the lake where you'll see Ole standing. For more information, visit www.www.alexandriamn.com or call 800-235-9441.

MISSISSIPPI

Biggest River
The Mississippi, Many States

The Mississippi winds 2,552 miles from the headwaters in Minnesota to the Gulf of Mexico, making it the largest river in North America. The river carries more than 400 million tons of cargo every year and provides water to more than 4 million people. Many of the cities along the river have an important relationship to the waterway. A system of 29 locks and dams controls navigation between Minneapolis and St. Louis on the upper Mississippi. The word Mississippi comes from the Algonquian word meaning "big water." Native American tribes who lived along the river included the Fox, Ojibwa, Winnebago, Choctaw, Natchez, and Yazoo. They farmed, traded, and named the river. Steamboats started traveling the river in the early 1800s. The Mississippi flows through channels cut out during the most recent Ice Age.

➨ **Directions:** The Mississippi gets its start in Northern Minnesota and winds all the way down to Louisiana, where it dumps into the Gulf of Mexico.

Smallest Woven Basket
Laurel, MS

According to the records at the Lauren Rogers Museum of Art, this is the smallest known Native American basket—a wee 1/16 of an inch wide and 1/24 of an inch tall. The basket is so tiny, the museum has a magnifying glass suspended above it so that visitors can more clearly see the detail.

Credit: Lauren Rogers Museum of Art

Jill Chancey, curator of the museum said the basket was made by Mary Benson, a Pomo Native American woman who is reputed to have crafted the basket in the early 1900s. Chancey said, Benson probably made the basket to show her skills as a weaver. A woman named Catherine Marshall Gardiner purchased the basket, and at the time, Benson had a second basket that was even smaller, which she didn't want to sell. The second basket has been lost to time. The small basket at the museum is the size of a plastic pin head. It's made of bulrush root and sedge grass.

The basket, and others in the collection, say much about the people, Chancey said. "They reflect both the weaver, the culture, and the geography," Chancey said. "Tribes used the material around them. It's a traditional Pomo bowl."

The tiny bowl has fascinated people for years. Visitors who haven't been to the museum in years will return and inquire about the basket.

"It's what kids remember more than anything," Chancey said. "It's one of our biggest—ironically—attractions."

➤ **Directions:** From Interstate 59, exit at 95C. Take a left at Beacon and follow the signs to the museum. Admission is free. The museum is open from 10 A.M. to 4:45 P.M. from Tuesday through Saturday and from 1 P.M. to 4 P.M. on Sundays. For more information, visit www.lrma.org or call 601-649-6374.

Largest Checkerboard
Petal, MS

The International Checker Hall of Fame is the home of the world's largest checker board—so large that you can use your body as a game piece. But you better be athletic if you want to king someone. In the Checker Hall of Fame, they actually use cushions for pieces. Or you can play a regular-size game. The Hall has a bust of Marion Tinsley, considered one of the all time checker playing greats.

➨ **Directions:** The Hall of Fame is located at 220 Lynn Ray Road in Petal, Mississippi. You typically need an appointment, at least one day in advance, to see the Hall, but you can visit for free. For more information, call 601-582-7090.

MISSOURI

Tallest Monument
St. Louis, MO

A Finnish-American architect won a national design competition in 1947–1948 for his idea for the Jefferson National Expansion Memorial—the Gateway Arch. His idea for the great arch was chosen as a fitting monument to the spirit of the Western pioneers. It was designed in part to celebrate the "soaring mind" of Thomas Jefferson, who encouraged a westward expansion of the United States. The Louisiana Purchase, which occurred under Jefferson's watch, doubled the size of the United States. Meriwether Lewis and William Clark set out from St. Louis in 1804 to explore the new land and report back. For a long time, St. Louis was considered the place where civilization ended and the unknown West began.

Eero Saarinen's design was said to be the most audacious of the 172 entries in the first competition. It started as a tribute to Jefferson and became a gateway to the west. It was delayed through the 1950s and 1960s as engineers and specialists studied the design. Saarinen, whose family immigrated to the U.S. when he was a teenager, died at the age of 51 in 1961 from a brain tumor, just as the construction on the arch began.

Author photo

His idea remains. The arch is 630 feet tall and the exterior is stainless steel. Construction began in 1963 and was completed in 1965 at a cost of $15 million. Its foundations are 60 feet into the ground. A tram takes visitors to the top in four minutes. (Only maintenance people are allowed to use the stairs.) The observation room at the top is six feet nine inches wide and will hold 160 people, according to the National Park Service. When the wind is blowing, the arch sways several inches from side to side—one inch for 20 mile per hour winds. Engineers say it can withstand any natural calamity; in 150 mile per hour winds, it should only sway 18 inches at the top.

Beneath the arch, underground, is the Museum of Westward Expansion, which details the Lewis and Clark expedition and has historical artifacts from the time.

➤ **Directions:** The Arch is located in downtown St. Louis on the bank of the Mississippi River. You can see it from miles away towering over the city. The arch is open daily from 8 A.M. to 10 P.M. Memorial Day through Labor Day and from 9 A.M. to 6 P.M. the remainder of the year. Admission to the museum is $3 and there is an additional charge for the tram ride ($5 adults) and a documentary movie ($4 adults.) For more information, visit www.nps.gov/jeff/ or call 314-655-1700.

Biggest Pecan
Brunswick, MO

When George and Elizabeth James started in the pecan business, the nuts were selling for three cents a pound. The family didn't start out as pecan farmers, but after a series of floods from the Missouri River ruined their crops in the 1940s, the family turned to pecans to make ends meet.

Author photo

In 1947, George, who passed away in 1998, found the Starking Hardy Giant pecan tree producing nuts he found large, oily, and delicious. Others followed, but James wanted to immortalize the Starking Hardy and so in the early 1980s, George made a replica of this particular nut.

The largest pecan is made of cement, steel beams, and chicken wire. It is as big as a camper van for the back of a truck. "People are fascinated by it," said his son, Bill James. "It has amounted to things no one envisioned."

His wife Elizabeth is still tending to the giant nut along with Bill. The James farm has 1,000 acres, with more than 10,000 unsprayed pecan trees. Pecan trees grow in Missouri naturally and many on the farm are more than 100 years old. They are harvested with a mechanical shaker and picked using two picking machines. They are then washed, cracked, and sold at the farm.

The James family has created an industry based not just on nuts, but on their big guy. Their fake pecan has been featured as a Trivial Pursuit board game question. Columnist Dave Barry has called with pecan questions. A store on the property, the Nut Hut, sells pecan fixings and a little history, including a scrap book of the James family farm. The walls are covered with articles about the family and the massive nut. There's even a 60-year-old pecan cracker. There are also pecan recipes and handy advice to refrigerate or freeze your nuts to keep them fresh.

➥ **Directions:** James' Pecan Farms Inc. is located on Highway 24, three miles east of the town of Brunswick. Signs on either side signal the farm. The pecan is visible from the highway. The shop is open seven days a week, from 10 A.M. to 2 P.M. most days but with longer hours after the harvest. For more information, call 660-548-3427.

Largest Goose
Sumner, MO

Located just a few flaps of the wings away from the Swan Lake National Wildlife Refuge, Sumner, Missouri is known by some as the "Wild Goose Capital of the World." To prove it, the town has a giant goose statue with a wingspan of 65 feet. The statue is made of fiberglass and is designed with its wings outspread so that it catches breezes and rotates in the wind. The statue is known by some as Maxi, short for Canadius Maximus.

➥ **Directions:** The goose is located in Sumner's city park. Sumner is located in north/central Missouri. From U.S. Highway 36, head south on Route 139. The main wildlife refuge entrance is one mile south of Sumner.

Largest Banjo
Branson, MO

Twang. The world's largest banjo is 62 feet long and a replica of the Gibson banjo. It's so big, it doesn't really fit in the room where it stays, so part of it sticks out the window. The banjo's 47-foot long neck has five fiber optic strings. It is 3,000 pounds of rockin' steel.

The banjo is on display at Grand Country Market, part of Grand Country area which includes hotels, restaurants, shows, miniature golf, and a water park.

➥ **Directions:** Grand Country Square is located at 1945 W. Highway 76 in Branson. The Market is open 9 A.M. to 10:30 P.M. daily. For more information, visit www.grandcountry.com or call 417-335-3535.

Largest Hairball
Jefferson City, MO

A visit to the Missouri Veterinary Museum reminds us of all that we don't know in the world. There was such a thing as hog cholera? How exactly does a giant cow hairball come out of a cow?

"A lot of times when they're gutted at the slaughterhouses, they just fall out," explains Schellie Blochberger, manager at the museum.

The hairball is more than six inches long and four inches wide and has a 12 inch circumference. It's oblong, of course, and you can see grain in it.

"We have a cat hair ball in here that's nice and smooth," said Blochberger. Founded in 1975, Missouri's veterinary museum is believed to be the oldest in the country.

➨ **Directions:** The Veterinary Museum is located at 2500 Country Club Drive in Jefferson City. Take 50 west to Route 179. Exit and turn right. Take the first right onto Country Club Drive and the museum will be at the end of the street on the left. Admission is free but donations are welcome. The museum is open from 9 A.M. to 4 P.M. Monday through Fridays and on Saturdays it's open by appointment. For more information, visit www.visitjeffersoncity.com or call 573-636-8737.

Largest Collection of Hair Art and Jewelry
Independence, MO

A wig from Dolly Parton? A fancy pony tail? No, that's not what goes into a hair museum. Leila Cohoon's hair museum has hundreds of wreathes and jewelry pieces containing or made of human hair. More than 2,000 pieces of jewelry and 160 framed hanging hair wreaths are on display. Many of them were made of human hair that is more than 100 years old. Wreaths made up of human hair were considered works of art during the Victorian times, especially in England. Families used to add hair to a wreath as their families grew.

The collection contains "needlework" type pictures made using hair instead of embroidery thread. Cohoon started collecting hair when she started Independence College of Cosmetology nearly 40 years ago.

➨ **Directions:** The museum is located at 815 W. 23rd Street in Independence. From Interstate 70, take Noland Road to 23rd Street. Turn left on 23rd and drive seven blocks to the museum. Admission is $3. The museum is open from 8:30 A.M. to 4:30 P.M. Monday through Saturday. Fore more information, visit www.hairwork.com/Leila/ or call 816-578-4606.

Largest Collection of Mosaic Art
St Louis, MO

Twenty different artists spent decades creating a mosaic so big it covers 83,000 square feet of the Cathedral Basilica of St. Louis. The installation contains more than 40 million pieces of small glass tiles. There are no paintings in the church—just mosaics.

They cover the ceilings and walls. They paint pictures of biblical history, of course, but also of the St. Louis Basilica, which was one of the first to racially integrate its schools. The mosaic project was begun in 1912 and not completed until 1988. The Mosaic Museum, on the lower level, offers additional information on the artwork.

Directions: The basilica is located at 4431 Lindell Boulevard in St. Louis. From Interstate 64/40, take Kingshighway Boulevard north to Lindell Boulevard. Turn right. Cathedral visiting hours are daily from 6 A.M. to 5 P.M. Tours are conducted from 10 A.M. to 3 P.M. For more information, visit www.cathedralstl.org or call 314-373-8200.

MONTANA

Smallest Town
Virgelle, MT

The question here is: Do two people constitute a town? Don Sorensen and Jimmy Griffin, the sole residents of Virgelle, Montana, aren't sure. At its height, Virgelle was home to a general store, a post office, a school, a bank, and a grain elevator. Today, Don and Jimmy have to travel 15 miles to get gas or groceries in Big Sandy. (The gas station closes early on Saturday and isn't open at all on Sunday.)

Virgelle was founded in 1912 by Virgil and Ella Blankenbaker, who built a general store. It was near railroad tracks and meant to be a hub for the area homesteaders, but farmland in the area wasn't lucrative. By 1930, only a few patrons were left to visit Virgelle Mercantile. Even so, the store remained in business until 1970 when the last owner shut it down.

In 1975, a pharmacist who grew up in the area reopened the Merc.

Today Don and Jimmy live there year round. They run the Virgelle Merc—a combined bed and breakfast, river outfitter, antique store, and a shuttle transportation company. In the summer they lead canoe and kayak trips on the Upper Missouri River and in the winter they sell antiques, at least until Christmas.

People always ask Don if he gets lonely.

"It's my home," said Don. " I grew up on a farm so I'm used to not having lots of people around." They have people coming to visit them all the time to take trips or buy antiques, which keeps them busy.

➤ **Directions:** Virgelle is 75 miles northeast of Great Falls. From Great Falls on Highway 87, go 12 miles past the town of Loma and watch for mile post 66. After you see the mile post 66, take the next gravel road on your right. Follow the sign toward "Missouri River Canoe Co. 8 miles." Follow the gravel road to the river bottom. When you pass through a concrete underpass, go right 1/8 mile to Virgelle. For more information, visit www.paddlemontana.com or call 800-426-2926.

Biggest Penguin
Cut Bank, MT

Ron Gustafson has experienced weather 48 degrees below zero in Cut Bank, Montana. In homage to the chilly weather, Gustafson built a 27-foot tall penguin outside his hotel, the Glacier Gateway Inn.

"Cut Bank a lot of times is known as the coldest spot in the nation," said Gustafson, who built the penguin in 1989. Fortunately, the temperature also changes pretty quickly. (The town next door is known for the greatest temperature change ever recorded within a 24 hour period.) The temperature in Browning, Montana dropped from 44 degrees Fahrenheit to negative 56 degrees Fahrenheit during one January day in the early 1900s.

➤ **Directions:** Glacier Gateway Inn is located at 1121 E. Railroad Street, on Highway 2 at the east end of Cut Bank. For more information, visit www.glaciergatewayinn.com or call 406-873-5544.

Tallest Smokestack
Anaconda, MT

The words are strangely incongruous: Smoke Stack State Park. And indeed, the area has a strange environmental history. This area has been a copper smelting plant, an Environmental Protection Agency Superfund site, and most recently, a golf course. The 585-foot tower was built in 1919. According to the state's tourism department, the Anaconda Company shut down its copper smelter in 1980, but the state legislature declared the tower a state monument in 1985.

According to the Environmental Protection Agency, milling and smelting in the area produced waste with high concentrations of arsenic, copper, lead, and zinc—which can lead to potential heath risks in humans and other things that are alive on the land and in the streams. In the 1980s, the EPA oversaw the smelter demolition and helped relocate families out of the Mill Creek area. The EPA and community have been working to restore the area ever since.

Directions: The park is located on Montana State Highway 1. There is no access to the tower. The viewing site for the smokestack is located at the junction of Park Street (Mt. Highway 1) and Monroe Street at the eastern edge of Anaconda. For more information, visit www.visitmt.com or call 406-542-5500.

NEBRASKA

Smallest Courthouse
Arthur, NE

Arthur, Nebraska is a beautiful little town of giant trees, green grass, and a large swing set. Just off the main highway, behind the new county building, is the historic Arthur County courthouse. In its heyday, it was home to the school superintendent, the county recorder, and a myriad of other positions in the 720 square mile county.

If you walk into the new courthouse or even just approach the door of the old one, you'll see a sign or someone will tell you it's possible to get a personal tour of the courthouse. If you're lucky to catch him, your guide is Ted Frye, an 80-plus gentleman who has been in Nebraska since homesteading was part of the daily conversation. Frye will give you a tour not only of the courthouse but also of the town's hay bail church which was built in 1928. It's been plastered over, but inside you can see a giant crack in the wall and the interior hay.

Frye wrote a history book on his town, and doesn't rush through

Author photo

his tour. Instead, he shares personal anecdotes of his life growing up around Arthur.

"All right, and so it was then," he begins many stories.

The courthouse is locked so you can't get in without a guide. Frye's been giving tours for more than five years and says he's had visitors from 14 different countries and nearly every American state.

The courthouse, he says, was used for about 50 years, between 1913 and 1961. The commissioners sold town lots to raise money for the building, which cost $900.

Legal business of setting up homesteads was conducted in two small rooms set up by the first county officers. The building has never had running water, but in 1925 the commissioners voted on getting electricity.

The building is still in good shape, despite chipping white paint around the 26 by 26 foot footprint of the building. Inside are rooms with wood floors and old fixtures from the courthouse's life: an old pencil sharpener, Nebraska law books, and a map from long ago. The city attorney's desk is in one corner, the school superintendent's desk in another.

"This corner was the sheriff's corner," Frye says. In another corner, sat the recorder's desk.

"That's where I bought my marriage license," Frye says.
Just outside is the old jail, with three scary cells.
There's no eating spot in town so bring your lunch.

➤ **Directions:** The courthouse is located on Main Street in Arthur, also known as State Route 61. The old courthouse is located behind the new county building.

Largest Porch Swing
Hebron, NE

It's not on a porch, but it does swing. This great porch swing sits in a lush park with big trees just a block or two from downtown Hebron.

The folks in Hebron wanted to make their town more apt for celebrations. One lady had seen people lining up in Kansas City just to sit in a four-seated swing. What would people do to sit on a swing that holds 16 people?

It was originally painted red white and blue when it was built in 1985.

➤ **Directions:** The porch swing is in Hebron, 48 miles south of York. From 81 southbound, head right or west on Lincoln. Head straight on the brick road until you see Fifth. Take a left on Fifth. The swing is at Roosevelt Park on the corner of Fifth and Jefferson. For more information, visit www.ci.hebron.ne.us or call 402-768-7156.

NEVADA

Largest Hotel
Las Vegas, NV

If you've ever been in the MGM Grand Hotel, you might have guessed it is not only the biggest in the country, but the biggest in the world. There's no need to go to the gym here, because you'll expend enough energy trying to figure out how to get to your room from the lobby. You can get married here, watch a live television show, eat in dozens of different restaurants, see live lions, sit in an arena watching a live boxing match or Hilary Duff, sin, float on an inner tube in a giant circle, and of course, win or lose a lifetime's worth of money all under one roof. The MGM has four

30-story towers and more than 5,000 rooms. We prefer the 3,000 square foot penthouse suites. Why bother going outside to see the rest of the city?

➡ **Directions:** The MGM is located on the Strip in Las Vegas, on the corner of Las Vegas Boulevard and Tropicana Avenue. From Interstate 15, exit at Tropicana and turn east towards the big buildings. For more information, visit www.mgmgrand.com or call 877-880-0880.

Largest Lit Hotel Sign
Las Vegas, NV

The hotels in Las Vegas earn a lot of superlatives. The most themed hotels in the world are here and the Las Vegas strip has the highest density of hotel rooms in the country. The biggest sign is not on the strip, however. The Las Vegas Hilton sign is the biggest lit sign in the country, measuring nearly 200 feet long and more than 30 feet tall.

➡ **Directions:** You can see it from across town, but for a closer look, the Las Vegas Hilton is located at 3000 Paradise Road. From Interstate 15, exit at Sahara Avenue and head east. Turn south on Paradise. For more information, visit www.lv-hilton.com or call 888-732-7117.

Largest Glass Sculpture
Las Vegas, NV

Every hotel in Las Vegas does it up. But the Bellagio has signed its name to a couple of key features. Included in its art collection, the Bellagio has the largest glass sculpture ever crafted. On the ceiling in the lobby is the Fiori di Como, a display of 2,000 hand-blown colorful glass flowers against a backdrop of light. The work was created by Dale Chihuly, who was commissioned by the Bellagio to create a piece in the lobby that would rival the aquarium at the Mirage. The final work is 2,100 square feet and weighs 40,000 pounds.

With more than 1,000 fountains outside their building, the Bellagio has the biggest collection at a hotel. They call it the "most ambitious, commanding water feature ever conceived." The choreographed fountains in front of the hotel dance to the music of noted entertainers including Frank Sinatra and the Mormon Tabernacle Choir. The fountains go off every 15-30 minutes, starting at 3 P.M. on weekdays and at noon on weekends.

➡ **Directions:** The Bellagio is on the Strip at the corner of Las Vegas Boulevard and Flamingo Road. From Interstate 15, exit at Flamingo

Road and head east. For more information, visit www.bellagio.com or www.chihuly.com or call 888-987-3456.

NEW HAMPSHIRE

Longest Candy Counter
Littleton, NH

Eight different kinds of black licorice. Gum Drops. Lollipops. M&M's separated by color. Candy lipstick. The joy of the world's largest candy counter comes in many colors and flavors. Carol Hamilton, who runs Chutters, says there are about 700 jars, spread out over a three-tiered candy counter in her store. That's 111 feet of different candies.

"There are no repeats," Hamilton says. She receives requests for unusual items and has tried to seek them out. The hardest requests are for the items no longer in production, like Turkish taffy, she says. Salted licorice? "It took me forever to find that," she says.

Hamilton once worked in nursing but changed to the candy business so

Author photo

that her days would be filled with more smiles. The store will celebrate its tenth anniversary in 2005.

There are plenty of substitutes if you can't find your favorite. There is true penny candy, where each piece costs one cent. Other candies are priced by the color of the label on their jar. Sugar free candies have a bright orange tag.

Chutters has bubble gum cigars, gummy teeth, and rock candy in various colors. Wax lips, lemon drops, circus peanuts, and sassafras slugs. They also have candy pebbles and coffee candies. Chutters also makes its own fudge.

➡ **Directions:** From Highway 91, exit at 41 and head towards downtown Littleton at 43 Main Street. The shop is open from 9 A.M. to 6 P.M. Monday through Thursday, 9 A.M. to 8 P.M. Friday and Saturday, and from 10 A.M. to 5 P.M. on Sunday. For more information, visit www.chutters.com or call 603-444-5787.

Windiest Spot
Mt. Washington, NH

The White Mountains are among the oldest in the United States, dating back 300 million years. The top of Mt. Washington is the highest point in the Northeast at 6,288 feet. Up there, the most ripping winds in the nation have been recorded. The world's fastest land wind velocity was clocked at 231 miles per hour in 1934. Mt. Washington State Park is 52 acres.

➡ **Directions:** Mt. Washington is located in the White Mountain National Forest in northern New Hampshire. A private road takes cars to the top from Highway 16, but it costs money to travel on it—$18 for one vehicle and driver and an additional $7 for anyone else in the car who's older than 12. You can pay to have a guided tour take you up for $24 per adult. The road is open from mid-May to October. Similarly, there's a railway that takes folks to the top, but there's a charge. You can hoof it on trails. The road is 8 miles to the top. The road was set up in 1861 as a carriage road. Follow Highway 16 and watch for signs leading to the peak. For more information, visit www.mt-washington .com or call 603-466-3988.

NEW JERSEY

Biggest Pipe Organ
Atlantic City, NJ

If the sounds of an organ just make you think of religious services, we're here to tell you those times are over. You can't get further from church here at the Atlantic City Boardwalk, not that this is a place where you should sin. We're saying that organs can be associated with sand, sun, and good times.

There are two organs at the Atlantic City Boardwalk Hall, (formerly known as Convention Hall). The world's largest pipe organ is located in the building's main auditorium. A second is located in the ballroom. The big one was built between 1929 and 1932, according to the folks at the Atlantic City Convention Hall Organ Society. The official number of pipes in the organ is 33,114; but experts believe there are probably more like 32,000.

➤ **Directions:** Boardwalk Hall is bound by Pacific, Georgia, and Mississippi avenues on the Boardwalk in Atlantic City. From the Atlantic City Expressway, follow signs for Pacific Avenue. Turn right on Pacific. For more information, visit www.acchos.org.

Oldest Original Lighthouse
Sandy Hook, NJ

According to the National Park Service, the lighthouse at Sandy Hook is the oldest standing light tower in the United States. It is not the first one ever built; there was a lighthouse built in Boston in 1716. But the light at Sandy Hook is the oldest one still standing and in operation. The light has beckoned boats into New York's harbor since 1764. Merchants in New York City requested the light be built to help sailors navigate the waters around Sandy Hook.

The state organized a lottery and later a 22 cent tax on ships to pay for the structure and its maintenance.

During the American Revolution, the light was put out in March of 1776 so the British couldn't navigate from it. Except during black-outs in World War II, the light has remained continuously lit. The original eight-sided tower is still in place. The walls are eight feet thick at the base and the tower is 85 feet tall. When the lighthouse was first built, it was located 500 feet from the northern end of Sandy Hook; now the light is more than half a mile from the point due to the change in the landscape over the years. It is maintained by the U.S. Coast Guard and still lights up the night, despite other lighthouses on the coast which are considered more important in the navigation of the area.

The light is located within Fort Hancock Military Reservation, directly south of New York City. Roughly ten feet from the tower is the former lightkeeper's house. Today it is an officer's quarters.

➤ **Directions:** In New Jersey, take State Highway 36 towards the beaches. The main park road runs up the finger of land that leads toward Sandy Hook lighthouse and Fort Hancock. Free tours of the lighthouse start at the Fort Hancock Museum. Children who attend must be at least 48 inches tall because the tour goes up 95 steps followed by climbing a ladder into the light area. For more information, visit www.nps.gov/gate or call 732-872-5970.

Biggest Light Bulb
Edison, NJ

Is there anything in our modern world so taken for granted as the incandescent light bulb? The good people of New Jersey are right to honor the little light creator and the man who created it. The Edison Memorial Tower was built in 1937 to honor Thomas Edison, the man who mastered incandescent light. Edison also patented the phonograph. The tower is located at the spot Edison had his laboratory.

➤ **Directions:** The light bulb, tower, and museum are located at 37 Christie Street in Menlo Park. The museum is open Tuesday through Saturday from 10 A.M. to 4 P.M. Admission is free. For more information, visit www.edisonnj.org/menlopark/ or call 732-549-3299.

NEW MEXICO

Largest Array of Radio Telescopes
Socorro, NM

While the name isn't very clever, the sight is truly impressive. The Very Large Array (VLA), as they call it, is 27 radio antennas configured in a Y-shape on the plains of western New Mexico. Each antenna is 82 feet in diameter. The data from each is collected and combined electronically. Construction of the VLA started in 1973 and the site was formally dedicated in 1980. It's been seen in movies such as *Contact,* where Jodi Foster uses the VLA to communicate with beings in space.

In reality, the VLA is used primarily by astronomers from all over the world to study the sun, planets, and other objects up there in the big world of space. Instead of attempting to explain how radio astronomy works here, I'll leave that to people who understand it.

➤ **Directions:** The VLA is located 50 miles west of Socorro on U.S. Highway 60. From 60, turn south on State Highway 52. Turn west on the VLA access road. The visitor center is open everyday from 8:30 A.M. to dusk. It contains videos and a small radio telescope to help explain how the operation works. You can also take a walking tour that leads toward one of the antennas. For more information, visit www.vla.nrao.edu or call 505-835-7243.

Biggest Roadrunner
Las Cruces, NM

Beep, Beep! Ah, yeah, you knew we were going to say that. The roadrunner is the state bird of New Mexico. Chances are if you look hard enough, you can find a coyote here too. This is the part of the country where these creatures live.

This 20-foot tall roadrunner was carefully constructed out of trash. Artist Olin S. Calk made the roadrunner out of garbage and other "found materials" around the Las Cruces area. He made it in 1991 as part of his work with schools and the community in recycling education. The roadrunner lived at the local dump for six years.

"People would come out to the landfill. Schools would come out to the landfill to see the bird," Calk says.

Prompting people to think about trash is part of the point. The breast of the bird is made of old tennis shoes. On the back are fishing rods, auto

Credit: Las Cruces Convention and Visitors Bureau

parts, toys, and pieces of trophies. The eyes are Volkswagen headlights and the beak is a galvanized trash can.

Calk said seeing it up close is a totally different experience than seeing it from Interstate 10.

"As you approach the work and become aware of what it's actually made of, that's the transition I enjoy watching," said Calk, who moved to New Mexico from Nashville. "Whether or not people get the message that the work is composed of discarded post consumer waste . . . some people get it and some people don't."

He made a roadrunner because of its connection to the Southwestern environment and after reading about Native American beliefs that say a roadrunner can lead a lost person out of the desert.

➤ **Directions:** The roadrunner is located off Interstate 10 at a rest stop about ten miles west of Las Cruces. You can only get into the rest stop from the eastbound lane, so if you're heading west, go to the next exit and turn around and come back on the east side.

Smallest Bride and Groom
Sandia Park, NM

Among what could be the world's largest collection of wedding cake couples is a wee couple who are here all the way from Mexico. Two fleas from Mexico are the world's smallest bride and groom. They were probably married sometime in the 1920s, because that's when their silk outfits were made. The fleas live in Tinkertown, a place created by artist Ross Ward, who passed away in 2002, but left his mark with his art. Tinkertown is filled with what Ward left behind, including miniature wood carvings and 50,000 glass bottles.

➡ **Directions:** The Tinkertown Museum is located in Sandia Park, which is just northeast of Albuquerque. From Interstate 40, take exit #175/Highway 14 north for six miles. Turn left on Highway 536 toward Sandia Crest. Tinkertown is 1.5 miles on the left. Tinkertown is open from April 1 through Nov. 1 daily from 9 A.M. to 6 P.M. Adult admission is $3. Kids from 4 to 16 get in for $1. For more information, visit www.tinkertown.com or call 505-281-5233.

Largest Gypsum Dune Field
Alamogordo, NM

They call it the White Sands National Monument, but it's not sand in the way we know it. The basin here is actually 275 square miles of gypsum—the world's largest such field. Gypsum is a typically white colored

Credit: National Park Service

mineral used to make sheet-rock and cement. The hillsides surrounding the valley are rich in gypsum. The gypsum was carried into the basin by rainwater running off the surrounding mountains. Neither the basin nor the river has an outlet, so the gypsum just sticks around, forming the dunes. Geologists at the park think the dunes are relatively young in earth terms. They have probably been here about 8,000 years. The dunes still move with the seasonal winds, which occur in March and April.

➤ **Directions:** White Sand Dunes National Monument is located outside Alamogordo. It can be reached from U.S. Highway 70. For more information, visit www.nps.gov/whsa or call 505-679-2599.

NEW YORK

Smallest Church
Oneida, NY

In the center of a small pond in Oneida, New York is a church so small, only two people can fit in it. The Cross Island Chapel was built in 1989 and measures 51″ by 81″ for a mere 28 square feet. It is nondenominational

Author photo

and open to the public on request. It is available for special occasions and several weddings have been performed here.

The church was built by Oneida residents Chandler Mason and his daughter Beth. Chandler passed away, but his memory lives on while his wife Janet and daughter take care of the church. Janet says Chandler originally built a big cross and someone suggested he build a church to go with it. They had heard of a small church in Maine where people had stolen pieces of the building, so they put it in the pond. It's accessible by boat and yes, people can fit in it.

"It's tall, it's just not very big," said Janet.

Directions: From Interstate 90, take exit 33 and head west on 365 for 2.5 miles. Turn right on Scononda Road and watch for the bend in the road at Mason Road. Turn right on Mason Road and the church is immediately on the right in the pond by the side of the road.

Largest Cathedral
New York, NY

The cornerstone of the St. John the Divine cathedral was set in 1892 and they say it is still not finished. Through the years, the cathedral has been through a lot. The New York design firm, Hans and LaFarge, won an international design competition with its Byzantine-Romanesque plan. The bronze doors were cast by Barbedienne of Paris, who cast the Statue of Liberty. Each door is 18-feet high and weighs three tons. The 40-foot diameter rose window in the west façade is the largest in the United States, and it contains more than 10,000 pieces of glass. The Christ figure at its center is life size at 5 foot 7 inches tall.

Author photo

The eight granite columns that surround the high altar were quarried on the island of Vinalhaven, Maine. Each is 55 feet tall. The two 12-foot Menorahs were gifts of Adolph

Ochs, the founder of *The New York Times*. Two painted enamel vases were gifts from Japanese Emperor Hirohito in 1926. The silver triptych, in the shape of a Russian icon, was created by Keith Haring in 1989.

The East End of the cathedral was dedicated in 1911 and the cornerstone for the nave was laid 14 years later. Its 601-foot length was unveiled in a dedication ceremony in 1941, one week before the bombing of Pearl Harbor. Construction was stopped and didn't resume until 1979. Then in 1994, construction of the South Tower stopped, and in 2001, a fire destroyed the North Transept. The restoration is an ongoing process.

➡ **Directions:** The church is located at 1047 Amsterdam Avenue at 112th Street in New York. For more information, visit www.stjohndivine.org or call 212-316-7540.

Largest Synagogue
New York, NY

According to Temple Emanu-El history, it was founded in 1845 by 33 German immigrants who came to the United States to escape the conservatism of Europe. They wanted to adapt their religious life to the new environment and a Reform congregation was born. It was the first Reform congregation in New York and the third in the nation. Today it is the largest synagogue in the world and home of the largest reform congregation.

The first place of worship was a rented room on Grand and Clinton streets on the Lower East Side. The congregation moved a couple times; and, as the congregation grew in prosperity, the idea of a big Temple grew. This site became the congregation's home in the 1920s. The property was formerly the site of the John Jacob Astor mansion. In September 1929, the first religious service was conducted, just weeks before the stock market crash.

It is an adaptation of the Moorish-Romanesque style. The main sanctuary can hold 2,500 people. A system of buttresses supports the interior space, which is 103 feet high, 77 feet wide and 147 feet long.

➡ **Directions:** The temple is located at the corner of Fifth Avenue and 65th Street. The temple is open for viewing from 10 A.M. to 4 P.M. Monday through Friday. For more information, visit www.emanuelnyc.org or call 212-744-1400.

Largest Internet Café
New York, NY

With light music, (Whitney Houston was heard on our visit,) you might actually be able to relax at the Easy Internet Café. This despite its central location in the middle of the crazy 24-hour Times Square atmosphere that is right outside the door. The café is more of a college-style computer room than a café. The business is a franchise with cafés all over Europe; this was the first outside Europe. There are rows of more than 600 PC's here, akin to a business call center. You pay for time at a kiosk and then help yourself to a computer. To keep you company, there's a food counter serving the ubiquitous New York soft pretzel and coffee.

➡ **Directions:** The café is located at 234 W. 42nd Street. Take a subway to Times Square. For more information, visit www.easyinternetcafe.com.

Oldest Piano
New York, NY

Inside the Metropolitan Museum of Art, there are probably hundreds of oldest, biggest, and most impressive things in the country. But we wanted to focus on one small part of the musical landscape. Bartolomeo Cristofor of Florence, Italy was the first to create a hammer action keyboard. If you look at this piano (which takes awhile to find in the huge Met) you can see it is surrounded by harpsichords, a toe-tapping instrument of that time. This model, made in 1720, resembles a harpsichord. The modern piano has evolved from his original creation.

➡ **Directions:** The piano is located in the Musical Instruments section of the Metropolitan Museum, which is located at 1000 Fifth Avenue. Suggested admission is $12 for adults and $7 for students and seniors. Children under 12 are free. This amount is the *recommended* admission price. If you are short on cash, the museum is just looking for a donation. You can get in for $1 if that is what you can afford to donate. The museum is closed Mondays. Hours are 9:30 A.M. to 5:30 P.M. Tuesday through Thursday and on Sunday. Friday and Saturday hours are 9:30 A.M. to 9 P.M. For more information, visit www.metmuseum.org or call 212-535-7710.

NORTH CAROLINA

Tallest Lighthouse
Cape Hatteras, NC

The Outer Banks of North Carolina sank hundreds of ships in the late 1800s and early 1900s. Cape Hatteras Lighthouse was built to help ships to navigate through this treacherous area. The tallest in the United States, its height has many different numbers attached to it. Some say 191 feet tall, others say 193 or 208 feet.

But according to the National Park Service Inventory of Historic Light Stations, this one is the tallest. The light was originally fueled by whale oil, but has been converted to use light bulbs. Its beam can be seen 24 nautical miles away.

The first lighthouse that was built in this area was 90 feet tall. It was shelled during the Civil War and replaced shortly thereafter. Its remains were visible until 1980 when a storm carried the rest away. The current lighthouse was built between 1868 and 1870. Roughly 100 local workers built it for a salary of $1.50 per day. Congress appropriated $167,000 for the construction.

It also holds the lighthouse world record for having been moved the furthest. The stripes on the light help identify the tower in the daylight. Different North Carolina lighthouses have different colors and stripes to mark them. At night, lighthouses can be differentiated by their different flashing rates. Mariners use tables that list lighthouse positions, markings, and intervals.

➡ **Directions:** The lighthouse is located at the eastern-most point of the seashore. Tours of the lighthouse are given seasonally—typically from early spring to Columbus Day in October. Tours usually sell out by noon. The ticket booth at the lighthouse opens at 8 A.M. daily. The last tour departs at 4:40 P.M. Tickets are $6 for adults and $3 for children and seniors. For more information, visit www.nps.gov/caha or call 252-473-2111.

Largest Ten Commandments
Murphy, NC

It's hard to remember these sometimes, especially on a road trip when you've been eating out of the back seat of your car for a few weeks. So take a step into all things biblical and reflect on all that is holy while in the

Credit: National Park Service

hillsides of North Carolina. Fields of the Wood began when Ambrose Jessup Tomlinson was praying on the hillside and had a vision. The idea to build the Church of God the Prophecy was revealed to him. He marked the place of his vision with 200 acres that the church bought near the spot. In 1945, the Ten Commandments were spelled out with concrete letters that are five feet tall and four feet wide. There's also the world's largest altar, the world's largest New Testament, and a concrete Bible that's 30 feet tall and 50 feet wide.

"It's a big spot in a little place," said Heath Ledford, who works in the gift shop.

➤ **Directions:** Fields of the Wood is at 10,000 Highway 294, 18 miles west of Murphy near the Tennessee line. For more information, visit www.fieldsofthewoodbiblepark.com or call 828-494-7855.

Biggest Chest of Drawers
High Point, NC

This 40-foot tall dresser even has a pair of wooden socks hanging out its front. The giant dresser doubles as a building. It was constructed in 1926 to call attention to the town as the "Home Furnishings Capital of the World," according to the High Point Convention and Visitors Association. It's been restored several times since, most recently as an eighteenth-century chest of drawers. The dresser holds clothes and the people wearing them; it has been serving as a home for the High Point Jaycees.

➤ **Directions:** The chest of drawers is located at 508. N. Hamilton Street in High Point, a city just southeast of Winston-Salem. From southbound U.S. 311, exit at #196 toward High Point. Go left on Westwood. Dresser is on the corner of Westwood and Hamilton. For more information, visit www.highpoint.org.

Biggest Highboy
Jamestown, NC

They must wear a lot of clothes in North Carolina. Within a quarter tank of gas of the High Point chest is the Jamestown highboy. This one is at the Furniture Land South campus. The highboy is 85 feet tall and was designed by a local furniture designer as a replica of one of the company's pieces—except this one is eleven times larger and tacked onto the side of the building.

➤ **Directions:** The big highboy is located at 5635 Riverdale Drive in Jamestown, a town just southwest of Greensboro. Heading southbound on Interstate 85, take the #118 exit/ Business Route 85 South. Travel for 2.5 miles. For more information, visit www.furnitureland south.com or call 336-841-4328.

Biggest Acorn
Raleigh, NC

In the community known as the City of Oaks, it all starts with a nut. But no small cheap nut will do for the city of Raleigh. In the center of town is a 1,250 pound, copper acorn. The acorn is considered good luck, and like the Blarney Stone, people want to touch it when they see it. It was built in 1991 as part of the city's bicentennial celebration. Every New Year's Eve, the city ceremoniously lowers the acorn to mark the start of the new year.

"It's fun to see something that is normally so small that large," said Terri Dollar, program director for Artsplosure, which helped construct the acorn. "People come from all over the place to rub it for good luck."

➤ **Directions:** The acorn is located in downtown Raleigh at Moore Square, on the corner of Blount and Martin streets. From northbound U.S. 401, turn right on Martin Street.

Biggest Shell
Winston-Salem, NC

The giant shell is the home of the Historic Preservation Foundation of North Carolina, which is a hint at the preservation value of the giant shell. According to Preservation North Carolina, it was built back in 1931 as one of eight shell-shaped Shell gas stations. Seven of the special stations were in Winston-Salem and the eighth was in the town next door. This one is the only one that remains. It was a gas station until the 1960s. Preservation North Carolina restored the building by chipping away at yellow paint and recreating the orange-yellow color of yesteryear's Shell. The wooden trellis that allowed cars to be washed and dried in the shade was reconstructed. Replica lamp posts and pumps were added to the site. The restoration was completed in 1997 and today the inside has two rooms, a bathroom, and offices for Preservation North Carolina. The Shell is only slightly larger than a child's playhouse.

➤ **Directions:** The Shell building is located at 1111 E. Sprague Street. From Interstate 40, take Highway 52 north. Exit at Sprague

Street and head east for one mile. The building is on the corner of Peachtree and Sprague. For more information, visit www.presnc.org or call 336-788-4772.

Oldest Coffee Pot
Winston-Salem, NC

In Winston-Salem stands what could be the matriarch of all superlatives—a giant coffee pot that dates back to 1858. Julius Mickey created the giant pot to attract customers to his tinsmith shop. According to Joyce Knabb at Old Salem, Inc., the coffee pot is seven feet tall and can hold 740 gallons of coffee. It's been painted and moved over the years and was relocated when Interstate 40 went in.

➨ **Directions:** The oldest coffee pot sits in a small grassy area at the intersection of Old Salem Road, Main Street and Brookstown Avenue. For more information, call 336-721-7300.

Longest Sit–In
Greensboro, NC

Okay, so the folks are not still sitting here, but we really like this building because it's such an important part of American history. It was here inside the Woolworth's Five and Dime that the longest sit-in occurred. It began on Feb. 1, 1960 when four African American freshmen from the North Carolina Agriculture and Technical College took a seat at the "all-whites" lunch counter. The four students ordered coffee and waited while the waitress and the manager ignored them. They had expected to be arrested, but that didn't happen. Some white customers taunted them and others whispered words of encouragement. When the store closed, they left, and returned the next day with more than a dozen supporters. And over the next week, the crowd of protesters grew to more than 400. The students demonstrated in shifts so that no one would miss their classes, and in the meantime, similar demonstrations sprung up in cities all over the south. The sit-ins continued for months until finally on July 25, four African Americans were served food at the Greensboro Woolworths counter. By the end of that summer, Greensboro and more than 30 other cities had integrated their lunch counters and restaurants.

➨ **Directions:** The Woolworths is located at 134 South Elm Street in the Northeast Shopping Center. It's being converted into a civil rights museum planned to open in February 2005. From southbound Interstate 85, take the East Lee Street exit and head west for roughly three miles into downtown Greensboro. Go right on Elm Street and head north for three blocks. The building will be on the corner of Elm and February One Place. For more information, visit www.sitinmovement.org or call 336-274-9199.

NORTH DAKOTA

Largest Buffalo
Jamestown, ND

You can see him from Interstate 90, overlooking Jamestown and a small herd of 30 bison that roam not far from his stationary stand. The buffalo was built by the local Chamber of Commerce, the idea of Harold Newman, then president. The sculptor was Elmer Paul Peterson, who was then an art instructor at Jamestown College. The sculpture was fabricated from eight-inch steel beaming, rods, wire mesh, and three inches of sprayed cement. It stands 26-feet tall and is 46 feet long. The 60-ton beast was made for $8,500 in 1959. Its dedication was attended by the governor, John Davis, and presidential candidate Nelson Rockefeller.

Author photo

Today it is the mascot of Frontier Village and the National Buffalo Museum, where you can visit a school house built in 1883 and a general store from 1878. The museum shows the history of bison (aka buffalo,) as well as Native American artifacts and art.

➤ **Directions:** From Interstate 94, exit at Highway 281/exit 258. Frontier Village is free and open in May and September from 10 A.M. to 5

P.M. In June, July and August, hours are 9 A.M. to 9 P.M. For more information, visit www.nationalbuffalomuseum.com or call 701-252-8648.

Biggest Holstein Cow
New Salem, ND

Among the superlative cattle in the Midwest states, Salem Sue is a doozy. She overlooks rolling fields dotted by rocks, probably left there by a retreating glacier. She represents her area, as do the New Salem High School students who are also known as the Holsteins. The cow is 38 feet high and 50 feet long. Salem Sue was built in 1974 at a cost of $40,000. She was funded by dairymen, farmers, businessmen, and area residents; but the New Salem Lions organized her construction and continue to maintain the site.

➤ **Directions:** From Interstate 94, exit 127. The cow is a half mile south of the freeway. Turn onto a dirt road and travel a half mile uphill to the base of the cow. Visitors are asked for a $1 donation for upkeep.

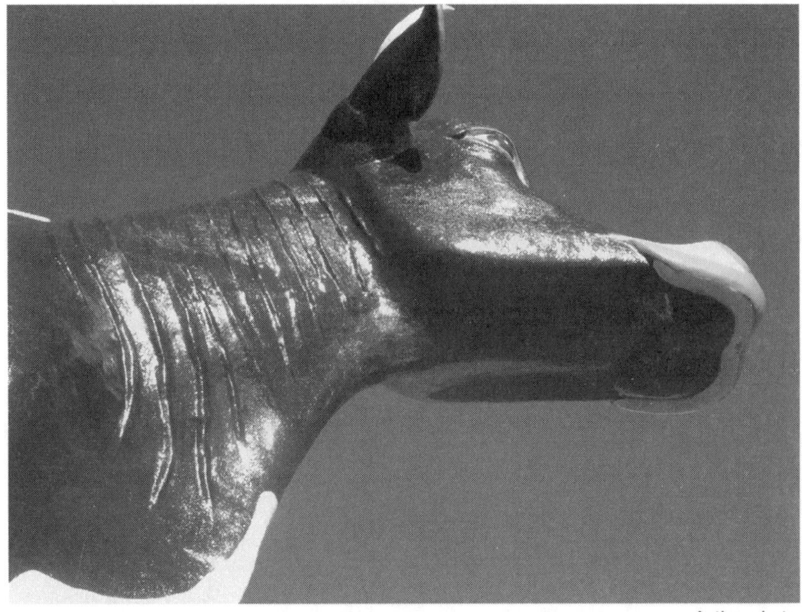

Author photo

Largest Scrap Metal Sculpture
Regent, ND

A sculpture called "Geese in Flight" begins the Enchanted Highway, a rolling road to Regent, North Dakota dotted with gigantic sculptures. The most visited is Geese in Flight, which towers over I-94 and is best seen from the westbound lanes. It's easily accessible from the freeway, and a row of little geese line the dirt road that takes you to the base of the sculpture. Once there you can get a good photo and learn a bit about the project along the road to Regent.

Gary Greff, a native of Regent, started building the sculptures as a way to encourage visitors to his hometown, which is 30 miles south of I-94. If you drive the route, you'll see a series of sculptures: "Deer Crossing", (4 miles from the Interstate); "Grasshopper" (15 miles from the Interstate); "Pheasants" (20 miles from the Interstate); "Teddy Roosevelt" (24 miles from the Interstate); and the "Tin Family" (27 miles from the Interstate). Each sculpture is just a few feet from the road and made with scrap metal found in industries from the plains area.

Author photo

At the end of the route is Regent, where there's gas, food, and a gift shop with a myriad of Enchanted Highway souvenirs from Enchanted Highway flying discs to flying metal geese you can stick in your back yard.

"Geese in Flight" was begun in 1998 and finished in 2002. It looks like a giant eyeball being circled by birds and is an awesome sight, towering over people, cars, and the landscape.

Along the route of sculptures, each work has a write up explaining some of its construction and ideas. "Deer Crossing", for example, shows a white tail and mule deer. The buck is 70 feet tall and the doe is 50 feet tall. Greff had cranes lift the two deer into flatbed trucks in order to move them to the site. On the way, he ran into a bit of trouble when he couldn't get the work past a narrow spot in the road. He had to cut the sculpture to get it to fit through and reweld it at the site.

"The Grasshoppers" were the fourth site in the series, added in 1999. Farmers have been tormented by these creatures (the real versions) but Greff said he wanted to build the sculpture to show their role in the history of North Dakota; farmers had to diversify their crops to deal with them.

"The Pheasants" sculpture took more than $3,000 in paint to complete. The "Tin Family", the first in the series, has feet made of livestock watering tanks. The 45-foot tall man has 16 telephone poles in his innards to hold him up.

The purpose of all the sites is to keep Regent alive, to inspire artistic expression, and to enhance the economic vitality of southwest North Dakota.

➡ **Directions:** At exit 72 off Interstate 94. "Geese in Flight" is yards from the freeway. The Enchanted Highway Gift Shop on Main Street in Regent is open everyday from Memorial Day to October from 9 A.M. to 6 P.M. For more information, visit www.enchantedhighway.net or call 701-563-6400.

Largest Sandhill Crane
Steele, ND

Majestic and stately, the giant sandhill crane of Steele, North Dakota is almost unnoticeable. He sits quietly next to a roaring freeway, making his image on the side of the road easy-to-miss. But he stands, illuminated, waiting to be seen.

According to the folks at the nearby Lone Steer Hotel, nesting ground of the giant crane, the 40 foot high crane was built by Jim Miller of Arena, North Dakota. A live sandhill crane is majestic and mysterious to the people who have seen them living in this part of the state. The sandhill crane is one of the oldest living species of birds. In real life, they are three to four feet tall and have a wingspan of six to seven feet—nearly giant in their own right.

➤ **Directions:** The big crane is located just north of Interstate 94 at the Steele exit. He's hiding behind the Lone Steer Motel Café at exit 200. For more information, visit www.lonesteer.com.

Biggest Catfish
Wahpeton, ND

Just past the Minnesota border, this giant fish is at home in what some Wahpeton residents call the best catch of the day, the Kidder Recreation Area. Here, next to the Red River, lives the "Wahpper," the world's largest catfish. You can catch one of your own by fishing from your own campsite

Author photo

in the park. And you know there's at least one fish here that won't get away.

➤ **Directions:** Kidder Recreation Area is on the south side of the Highway 210 bypass. From 4th Street North, turn on Dabill Road. Drive behind the city hall into the park until you can go no further. You'll see the fish near the river. You can also see him from 210 near a giant cell tower. For more information, visit www.wahpeton.com.

OHIO

Biggest Rubber Stamp
Cleveland, OH

It looks like an innocent, big piece of public art. But the "Free Stamp" of Cleveland, Ohio has caused some commotion in its life. This is another

Author photo

example of the gigantic work of Claes Oldenburg and Coosje van Bruggen, who have created "Large-Scale Projects" like this one all over the United States, Spain (a giant pocket knife with oars,) France (a giant partially buried bicycle,) and Tokyo (a giant saw.) (See Minnesota superlatives for information on their giant spoon in Minneapolis.)

According to the city of Cleveland's Web site, this is one of the most controversial works of art in the city. While some love it as a work of pop art, others think it's an eyesore. The debate started when the work was commissioned in 1982. Standard Oil wanted a piece of modern art for the Public Square near their offices. The artists checked out the spot where their work would go and proposed an enormous stamp. They decided on the word "free," according to the city, as a statement of liberty and independence. Before the work was completed, new managers at Standard Oil of Ohio disagreed with the idea of a giant rubber stamp in the Public Square. They asked the artists to consider a new location. Different spots around the city were entertained and debated. Production of the stamp halted and its pieces were stored in Indiana. Members of the City Council didn't want it in Willard Park, even though the artists thought of the location as part of their artistic expression.

Cleveland had a new mayor and new city council president before the issue was resolved and the artwork was placed in Willard Park. The artists changed the design so that the stamp appeared to be falling over, representing the history of the stamp being tossed from the Public Square into the park. It was dedicated in 1991.

➥ **Directions:** The stamp is outdoors in downtown Cleveland in Willard Park, just up the hill from the Rock and Roll Hall of Fame. The park is at the corner of East 9th Street and Lakeside, next to Cleveland City Hall. For more information, visit www.city.cleveland.oh.us.

Largest Cuckoo Clock
Wilmot, OH

A German immigrant began building the clock in 1962 but died before he finished. The finished product took 12 years to complete and it stands 23–1/2 feet tall and 24 feet long. The figures were hand-carved and imported from the German Black Forest. An Amish carpenter living next door finished the project, which includes gnomes relaxing under a giant clock. The cuckoo is as big as a detached garage, a kind of shrine to time. Deer, dancing people, yellow flowers, and trees adorn the clock, along with birds that rock back and forth with the ticking of seconds.

The clock dings every half hour, with gongs marking the time at the top of every hour.

The clock was on the cover of the *Guinness Book of World Records* in the 1970s, but at the time there was no cuckoo competition in the book, according to managers of the restaurant.

In the 1930s, the site was originally a milk co-op and later, a cheese factory. Today, it's a restaurant and gift shop.

➡ **Directions:** The clock is outside on the roof of Grandma's Alpine Homestead restaurant. It's not accessible in the winter or when the restaurant is closed. Grandma's Alpine Homestead restaurant is located between Wilmot and Winesburg on Highway 62. For more information, visit www.millerhaus.com or call 330-359-5454.

Largest Amish Buggy
Berlin, OH

This buggy is so special, it's never even been outside. The shop where the buggy is housed has a craft shop inside. The buggy was built there, and it still lives inside. The shop had the buggy built when it opened in 1994 and it has never left the store. The front wheel is five-feet tall and the black buggy weighs 1200 pounds . . . maybe what an Amish Arnold Schwarzenegger might drive. Indeed, it matches Amish buggies that you might see on the roads around Holmes County, which is home to the largest Amish population in the world. Nearly 35,000 Amish people live here. The Amish culture shuns many modern conveniences most of us can't imagine living without: television, radio, insurance. The idea is to live separately from the world. It reflects a respect for tradition and a belief in nonconforming to the ways of the world which might lead to temptations and away from community and family life. There is an interesting melding of two cultures around the Berlin area.

Amish people have their roots in the Mennonite community in Europe. In the late 1600s, a Swiss bishop named Jacob Amman broke from the Mennonite church and his followers were called the Amish. Amish people immigrated to North America in the early eighteenth century.

➡ **Directions:** The Wendell August Gift Shoppe and Forge is located at 7007 Dutch Country Lane on Highway 62 just east of Berlin, under a blue and yellow striped water tower. The buggy is inside the shop, so you'll have to go when the shop is open to see it. Summer hours are Monday through Saturday from 9 A.M. to 6 P.M. with truncated hours in the winter months. For more information, visit www.wendellaugust.com or call 330-893-3713.

Biggest Basket
Newark, OH

There are certain things in the world that you look for long before you can actually see them: the ocean after a long drive, the Grand Canyon on your first drive across the Northern Arizona landscape, and the Longaberger basket. It juts out of the horizon like a mountain—a seven story office building that is shaped like a basket. In the immortal words of Longaberger founder Dave Longaberger, "If they can put a man on the moon, they can certainly build a building that's shaped like a basket."

This is the Longaberger corporate headquarters. Longaberger builds high end baskets, which are sold sort of like Avon or Tupperware—by people in their homes. You can visit a retail store and factory at the "Longaberger Homestead," which is 17 miles from the building basket. The Longaberger Company designed the building and trademarked it. Ground-

Author photo

breaking was in October 1995 and the basket employees moved in two years later. The building sits on a 25 acre campus and 500 employees can work inside the basket's 180,000 square foot interior.

Two basket handles are attached to the top of the building. They are heated during the winter to prevent ice from forming and crashing down on the glass ceiling over the building's atrium. Two Longaberger tags are attached to the side of the building; each weighs 725 pounds.

There are no tours, but you can enter the atrium of the building and look up to see the glass ceiling and the giant handles overhead. The lobby also has product displays and the Longaberger sales kit for the independent home consultant business opportunity.

➡ **Directions:** The Longaberger Home Office is located on 1500 E. Main Street in Newark. You drive past the building campus on State Highway 16. To get inside, from the highway, turn on Dayton and then on Main. For more information, visit www.longaberger.com or call 740-322-5588.

Tallest Roller Coaster
Sandusky, OH

In 2003, Cedar Point opened the Top Thrill Dragster, a white knuckle coaster that is the tallest in the world. The coaster reaches 420 feet tall and tops out at 120 miles per hour, enough to make you glad you're alive once you get back on stable ground. The coaster begins at a "starting line," where you rev your carriage before hitting 120 miles per hour in about four seconds. The train zooms straight up the big hill on a track that rotates 90 degrees and then falls down, down, down. The coaster was designed by Intamin AG of Wollerau, Switzerland. It has 2,800 feet of track and a hydraulic launch system. The train has tiered seating (similar to stadium seating) so that you can see the plunge you are about to take. It is the first coaster to top 400 feet and the first to reach speeds of 120 miles per hour.

➡ **Directions:** Cedar Point is located on the Lake Erie Peninsula in Sandusky, Ohio. All day admission in 2004 was $43.95 for anyone older than age 3. Take U.S. Interstate 250 and follow the signs to the Cedar Point Causeway. The park has different hours depending on the season, so call ahead. For more information, visit www.cedarpoint.com or call 419-627-2350.

Oldest Concrete Pavement
Bellefontaine, OH

Ah, concrete. Where would we be without it? It's given us sidewalks, foundations, and walls. The first concrete streets started here in Bellefontaine, where in the late 1800s, traffic buzzed with buggies and horses. People were looking for an alternative to muddy and dusty dirt streets. George Bartholomew had an idea—pavement. He had an idea for "artificial stone" and started making it as the Buckeye Portland Cement Co. The street was so avant-garde at the time, that Bartholomew won an engineering award for it. He pitched the idea to the city. According to the Logan County Historical Society, the city allowed Batholomew to pave a small section by the Logan County Courthouse. The idea was considered risky at the time, so the city required a $5,000 bond when it was installed. When the street didn't fall apart, all the streets around the courthouse square were paved. On the street's 100th birthday, the city closed Court Street in 1991 to preserve the area, but residents wanted to drive to the courthouse. It was reopened in 1998 to traffic. The town also has a statue of one of the men who helped get it—George Bartholomew.

➤ **Directions:** The concrete is at the corner of Opera and Court streets near the courthouse. Highway 68 turns into Main Street which intersects with Court Street. For more information, visit www.co.logan.oh.us.

OKLAHOMA

Largest Curio Cabinet
Clinton, OK

So many curios live in the cabinet of Pat Smith's Oklahoma Route 66 Museum, she's not even sure how many she's got in there. The curio extravaganza is 12 feet by 16 feet of glasses, ceramics, mugs, and other collectibles to help you get your kicks on this former segment of Route 66. Smith has been collecting memorabilia from Route 66 for her museum, which chronicles the old road in rooms that are themed by the decades. Starting in the 1920s, each room tells the story of a different ten-year period, including Native American art and displays from the Mohawk Lodge.

➡ **Directions:** The Oklahoma Route 66 Museum is located at 2229 W. Gary Boulevard. From Interstate 40, take exit 65 and get on the Gary Freeway. Summer hours are 9 A.M. to 7 P.M. Monday through Saturday, and 1 P.M. to 6 P.M. on Sunday. For more information, visit www.route66.org or call 580-323-7866.

Biggest Dick Tracy Cartoon
Pawnee, OK

Chester Gould, the creator of Dick Tracy cartoons, was born in Pawnee, Oklahoma. The town has honored him with a giant 20 foot by 20 foot cartoon of Dick Tracy on the corner of 6th and Harrison in downtown Pawnee. Gould left Oklahoma for Illinois, where he studied cartooning and then created cartoons for newspapers. His creation was first distributed in the 1930s as one of the first detective/cops/robbers cartoons. The old timers in Pawnee say that in the original cartoon, the Pawnee townspeople were identifiable in Gould's characters.

➡ **Directions:** Pawnee is roughly 60 miles northwest of Tulsa. U.S. Highway 64 goes through Harrison, the home of the Dick Tracy cartoon.

Highest Hill
Poteau, OK

Cavanal Hill near Poteau, Oklahoma claims to be the country's highest hill. It measures 1,999 feet, one foot shy of being categorized as a mountain. The story goes that some Boy Scouts back in the 1930s were corresponding with scouts in England when they learned the factoid, according to Patti Curry at the Poteau Chamber of Commerce. The English scouts told the American scouts that their town was home to the tallest hill; the English scouts had read it in their scouting handbook. The story has stuck around, and today the town has events centered around and on the hill, including a five-mile run and bike riding events.

➡ **Directions:** Poteau is located on the eastern side of Oklahoma, near the Arkansas border. From Highway 59/271, get on Smith Road, which turns into Mockingbird Lane. Turn on Witteville Drive and head up the hill. For more information, visit www.poteau.org.

OREGON

Largest Wooden Structure
Tillamook, OR

It's in Oregon and it's not even a tree. The hangar at the Tillamook Air Museum was built in 1943 to shelter blimps used for anti-submarine patrols during World War II. Today it is home to a private aircraft collection and remains a formidable sight that dwarfs its contents. From the outside it looks like your average big building, but on the inside, looking up at the wooden planks of the ceiling and walls, you get an appreciation of its great size. The building is 1,072 feet long with a total area of seven acres—big enough to play six football games simultaneously.

According to the air museum, the U.S. Navy began construction in 1942 on 17 wooden hangars to house the blimps. The fleet of blimps patrolled the coast and served as convoy escorts. Two hangars were built in the Naval Air Station Tillamook to serve the Washington and Oregon coasts, but one of the hangars was destroyed by fire in 1992.

Eight airships were originally stored here. Each was 252 feet long and filled with 425,000 cubic feet of helium. They could stay up in the air for three days and fly 2,000 miles.

The Tillamook air station was decommissioned in 1948. Since 1994, the remaining hangar has been home to a privately owned aircraft collection which contains a long list of airplanes.

Directions: If you're flying, you can taxi right up to the hangar. If you're driving, the Tillamook Air Museum is located two miles south of Tillamook on Highway 101. The museum is open daily except for Thanksgiving and Dec. 25. Summer hours are 9 A.M. to 6 P.M. Adult admission is $10.50. Children between the ages of 6 and 17 get in for $6. For more information, visit www.tillamookair.com or call 503-842-1130.

Smallest City Park
Mill Ends, Portland, OR

Some believe that leprechauns live in the tiny park in downtown Portland. A newspaper columnist named Dick Fagan (1911-1969) could see this small plot of land from his Front Avenue office window at the *Oregon Journal.* (Front is now called Naito and the Oregon Journal isn't around anymore.) According to the story, as told by Portland Parks and Recreation, the city was supposed to erect a light pole on the little plot of land, but when it never appeared, Fagen started writing about the events of the small space, which he called the world's smallest park.

His column was called "Mill Ends", the name given to leftovers at lumber mills. In his pieces he wrote about a head leprechaun named Patrick O'Toole who was seen only by Fagan. (He wrote that it was the only such colony west of the Emerald isles.)

His readers contributed gifts to the park, including a swimming pool and diving board for butterflies. Real weddings and bagpipe concerts have been held at the park. The site was dedicated an official Portland city park on St. Patrick's Day in 1976.

Author photo

➥ **Directions:** The park is 452 square inches and sits casually in the median of southwest Naito Parkway and Taylor streets downtown in the public right of way. For more information, visit www.parks.ci.portland.or.us or call 503-823-7529.

Longest Hobby Miniature Railway
Chiloquin, OR

Quentin Breen and his friends started building the railway line 15 years ago, and today there are 25 miles of track at the Train Mountain Railroad Museum. It's big enough that you can ride on it, and Breen takes visitors on nine minute rides. The railway is located at the Train Mountain Railroad Museum, a non-profit organization aimed at preserving railroad heritage.

➥ **Directions:** Train Mountain is located in the southern Oregon town of Chiloquin, in between Klamath Falls and Crater Lake. The entrance is on 36941 South Chiloquin Road. From U.S. 97, turn right on Chiloquin Road. Train rides are available every Sunday during the summer, between Memorial Day and Labor Day from 10 A.M. to 3 P.M. There's no admission fee but donations are welcome. For more information, visit www.trainmountain.org or call 541-783-3030.

Biggest Sea Cave
Florence, OR

Wooden steps brought people down to these caves in the 1800s and you can still see remnants of those stairs scattered on the ground. Today you have to take an elevator from Highway 101 down to sea level just to get in. As cool as the sea caves are, even cooler are the sounds of the boisterous sea lions barking inside the cave and the rush of the waves against the walls of the cave. (Imitating these creatures provides hours of the fun in the car later, for you at least, if not for your friends.) The herd averages 200 members and the sea lions are in the area year round, but they are in the cave more in the winter and fall.

The cavern probably began forming 25 million years ago, the folks at the cave say. It is as high as a 12-story building and the length of a football field. From the cave entrance you can see the Heceta Head lighthouse, said to be one of the most photographed beacons in the country. The lighthouse was built in 1893 and is the strongest light on the Oregon Coast. You can tour the lighthouse and sleep in the Heceta house, where the lightkeepers once lived.

➤ **Directions:** The Sea Lion Caves are on the central Oregon coast, 11 miles north of Florence on Highway 101. The cave is open every day, except December 25, at 9 A.M. Closing time varies with the season, depending on sundown. Admission is $7.50 for adults and $4.50 for children between the ages of six and 15. For more information, visit www.sealioncaves.com or call 541-547-3111.

Deepest Lake
Crater Lake, OR

With nearly 2,000 feet between the surface and the bottom, Crater Lake is the deepest lake in the country and the seventh deepest in the world. The lake is in the middle of a volcano's crater, or caldera. The mountain that was once here, Mt. Mazama, collapsed after an eruption nearly 8,000 years ago.

The Native Americans of the region, the Klamath, tell the legend of the eruption as a war between two chiefs. One chief, Llao, was the god of the

Credit: National Park Service

Below World. The other, Skell, was from the Above World. Their battle was so fierce, it resulted with the destruction of Llao's home, Mt. Mazama.

The five-mile wide caldera remains. Filled with water from snow and rain, it is now Crater Lake. The average snow fall of Crater Lake is 533 inches per year—some of the heaviest in the country. The clean water and the lake's depth help make the lake an electric blue color.

Directions: The park is always open but many roads and facilities close for the winter. Routes 138 and 62 lead into the park. The North Entrance station is only open in summer. The Rim Village Visitor Center is open from June through September from 9:30 A.M. to 5 P.M. The Steel Visitor Center is open all year, with summer hours of 9 A.M. to 5 P.M. Admission is $10 per vehicle. For more information, visit www.nps.gov/crla or call 541-594-3000.

Longest Wingspan on an Airplane
McMinnville, OR

They call it the Spruce Goose because it's made out of wood, mostly birch. The "Hughes Flying Boat" was designed to transport cargo and soldiers over long distances during World War II. People wanted an option safer than boats, which were vulnerable on the open seas.

Builder Henry Kaiser teamed up with Howard Hughes to propose a fleet of fliers. Their corporation won an $18 million government contract to build three of the flying ships.

Hughes's team designed a plane that could carry 750 troops. They named it the HK-1, after themselves and their first design. The government required that the designers of the plane not use material important to the war effort, such as steel and aluminum, so they used wood. This requirement that the giant plane be made of wood caused several delays. Kaiser eventually withdrew from the project, and the plane was eventually named H-4, reflecting Hughes's name and the number of designs. When the war ended and the plane was still not in the air, people were increasingly vocal about the long, expensive government project. The U.S. Senate wanted to know if its funds were misspent and called Hughes to Washington to testify. Finally, in 1947, people gathered to see Hughes fly the completed plane for 90 seconds over the water of the Long Beach California Harbor. It was the only time the plane was flown. The plane was stored for decades and not displayed again until after Hughes died. In the 1980s it was displayed to the public in a southern California exhibit. In 1990, Evergreen Aviation in Oregon won the rights to display the plane. The plane was taken apart and moved by barge up to Oregon. Years would pass before the plane was rebuilt. While in storage, the Spruce Goose was restored and a giant hangar was built in McMinnville to showcase the plane. The plane faces a giant glass window so that passersby can see it from the roadway out front. The new museum opened on D-Day 2001, displaying the largest wooden plane ever built. It has a wingspan of 319 feet 11 inches, which covers an area of more than 11,000 square feet.

➡ **Directions:** The Evergreen Aviation Museum is located at 500 NE Capt. Michael King Smith Way, just off Highway 18. Admission is $11 for adults and $7 for children ages six through 18 and students with identification. The museum is open everyday except Thanksgiving, December 25, and January 1. For more information, visit www.sprucegoose.org or call 503-434-4180.

Tallest Barber Shop Pole
Forest Grove, OR

Don't expect it to light up, spin, or have a barber anywhere nearby. The world's largest barber pole in Forest Grove is really just a painted telephone pole. The 72-foot tall beauty is meant to encourage singing in barbershop quartets.

➨ **Directions:** Forest Grove lies at the western edge of the Portland suburbs. From U.S. 26, take Highway 47 south to Willamina Avenue. Turn west/right on Willamina, then left on Main Street. The pole is located on the west side of the baseball fields at Lincoln Park, just off Main Street.

Biggest Rabbit
Aloha, OR

This guy used to be one of the Texaco Service Men, but a couple of big ears changed him to a rabbit in a blue jacket. He greets visitors to Harvey Marine, a boat shop in the western suburbs of Portland.

➨ **Directions:** Harvey is located at 21250 SW Tualatin Valley Highway in front of Harvey Marine. From U.S. 26, take the Murray Boulevard exit 67. Go left on Murray. Go right on Tualatin Valley Highway. Drive 3.5 miles to the bunny.

Shortest River
Lincoln City, OR

The shortest river is so short, it doesn't even have a whole name. They call it the D River, and it vies with Montana's Roe River for the smallest in the country. The Roe, which starts from Great Springs near Great Falls, Montana, is 201 feet long before it flows into the Missouri River. The D River in Oregon claims to be the shortest river in the world at a mere 120 feet. It flows from Devil's Lake into the Pacific Ocean.

➨ **Directions:** The D River State Recreation Site is on U.S. Highway 101, just north of Lincoln City. Watch for signs for the park from 101, south of the State Highway 18 junction. For more information, visit www.oregonstateparks.org or call 800-551-6949.

PENNSYLVANIA

Oldest Still-Operating Drive-In Movie Theater
Orefield, PA

Tucked into a residential neighborhood with a small-town feel, Shankweiler's Drive-In Theater is a gem of a little movie theater. It has grass, gravel, one screen, and is surrounded by houses. It has been showing movies under the night skies since 1934. According to the theater's history, it was the second drive-in the in the United States. As the times changed, the drive-in became more technologically advanced; in 1948, speaker poles and car speakers were installed; new screen, snack bar, and projection rooms were built in 1955 after a hurricane leveled the buildings on the property. In 1982, AM radio broadcasting came to the theater; in 1986, the movie sounds could be heard on the FM dial; and in 2002, the FM system was updated. Just remember to keep your foot off the brake pedal.

➤ **Directions:** Shankweiler's is just outside Allentown at 4540 Shankweiler Road in Orefield, Pennsylvania. From I-78, take Route 309 (exit 53) north for nine miles. Turn left at Shankweiler Road. The Theater is generally open on weekends in April and May, and seven days a week from June through Labor Day. Sometimes Shankweiler's is open on weekends in September. Adult admission is $6 for adults and $3 for children between the ages of 3 and 12. For more information, visit www.shankweilers.com or call 610-481-0800 for 24 hour information.

Largest Mint
Philadelphia, PA

At the U.S. Mint, it's all about coinage. The mission of the mint is to produce the right amount of money so that the nation can do business. According to the U.S. Mint, this has meant a circulation that has varied in recent history, from 11 billion to 20 billion coins annually. Interestingly, the Mint is a self-funded agency, so any revenues it makes over its operating expenses are turned over to the General Fund of the Treasury. We're not sure if they pay in coins.

In addition to making coins, the Mint is also responsible for custody and protection of the country's $100 billion of gold and silver. Paper currency is not made here; it's produced at the Bureau of Printing and Engraving. But the Philadelphia Mint is not only the biggest in the country; it's the biggest in the world.

➤ **Directions:** The Mint entrance is at Arch and Fifth streets in old downtown Philadelphia. Tours are scheduled in advance and available only to select groups such as school children and military/veterans groups. Call 215-408-0114 or visit www.usmint.gov for more information.

Largest Crayon
Easton, PA

They call it the colossal Crayola, and it was created from the left-over crayons from kids all over the country. Crayola got blue "leftovers" from kids and melted them all together to form the world's biggest crayon, which is on display in the Crayola Store. The crayon is 15 feet long and weighs nearly 1,500 pounds.

➤ **Directions:** The Crayola store is located next to the Crayola FACTORY (which they spell with all capital letters and is not actually where their crayons are manufactured) in downtown Easton. From Interstate 78, take exit 14 toward Easton. Turn right on Morgan Hill Road. Bear right at Philadelphia Road. Turn left at St. John Street. Cross the bridge, staying in the middle lane and go straight onto Third Street. Turn left on Pine Street and you should be there. The store is located outside the tour center and open Monday through Saturday from 9 A.M. to 6 P.M., and Sunday from noon to 6 P.M. For more information, visit www.crayola.com/factory/ or call 888-827-2966.

RHODE ISLAND

Smallest State

On a long road trip, Rhode Island can be a welcome sight because you can drive across the whole state in less than an hour. From north to south, Rhode Island is 48 miles long. And from east to west, it's 37 miles across. The whole place is just over 1,200 square miles.

➤ **Directions:** Rhode Island is on the east coast between Massachusetts and Connecticut.

Oldest Carousel
Watch Hill, RI

With real horse hair mane and tail, the Flying Horse carousel is about as close as you can get to a bronco without any bucking. The carousel at Watch Hill is considered the oldest in the country, dating back to at least 1876, according to Rhode Island historians. The carousel has 20 original horses which are not secured into a platform. Instead, they are suspended from above, hanging from chains. The faster the carousel turns, the more air the horse catches. The rider is swung and hence the carousel is known as the flying horse. The National Carousel Association says thousands of wooden carousels were carved in the United States between 1885 and 1930, but fewer than 150 remain today. Each horse on the Watch Hill carousel is hand carved from a single piece of wood and they wear real leather saddles. Rhode Island tourism officials say this carousel came to the state in 1879 when a traveling carnival abandoned it here. The carousel charges 50 cents for a ride on the inside horses. Riding the outside horses costs $1 because you have a chance of winning a free ride.

➡ **Directions:** The Flying Horse Carousel is located at 153 Bay Street in Watch Hill, which is at the southwestern tip of Rhode Island. From Interstate 95, get on Route 2 or Route 3 to Route 78 toward the beaches. From 78, take a left on Watch Hill Road which will lead to Bay Street. The carousel is open during summer months from 11 A.M. to 9 P.M. Monday through Friday, and from 10 A.M. to 9 P.M. on Saturday and Sunday. The carousel is stored during winter months. For more information, visit www.visitwatchhill.com or call 401-348-6007.

Giant Rosary
Newport, RI

Every year from May until October, Jesus Saviour Church wears a rosary. The "beads" are made of buoys. And the cross hangs over the front door. The rosary is lit in May and October to honor Mary.

➡ **Directions:** The giant rosary beads are located at Jesus Saviour Church, at 509 Broadway in Newport. For more information, visit www.jsaviour.org or call 401-846-4095.

Biggest Termite
Providence, RI

If you are a follower of big things out there in the bug world, you know that there are big things that attract big attention and big things that attract little attention. The Big Blue Bug in Providence, Rhode Island could be the king of all marketing giants. From the website, www.bluebug.com to the phone number, 800-BLUEBUG, New England Pest Control has taken this bug and flown with him. Nibbles is his first name. Woodaway is his last. He has been a part of the pest control operation since 1980. He is savvy to the changing seasons and dresses up for holidays. He's a witch on Halloween and Uncle Sam on July 4. Nibbles is nine feet tall and 58 feet long and he has four wings that are each 40 feet long. His influence has been felt far and wide. He's spawned t-shirts, plush toys, web cams, and even prompted a Rhode Island woman to have an image of Nibbles tattooed on her leg.

➨ **Directions:** Nibbles is visible from Interstate 95. His home is at 161 O'Connell Street. For a closer look, from I-95, take exit 19. Take a left at Eddy Street and another left on O'Connell Street. For more information, visit www.bluebug.com or call 888-BLUEBUG.

SOUTH CAROLINA

Biggest Peach
Gaffney, SC

Yes, it's a water tower, but it has a cleft just like a real peach and even a little leaf! The people of South Carolina really want you to know that their state produces more peaches than that southern state with the peach on its license plates. The Board of Public Works in Gaffney built "The Peachoid" in 1981.

They say the idea came at a board meeting late one night when the board was brainstorming ways to get federal funding for a new water tower. It took five months to design and mold the steel. Fifty gallons of paint were needed to cover it. The peach leaf is 60 feet long and 16 feet wide. The orange giant holds a million gallons of water. You can get a postcard of it at the South Carolina Welcoming Center on Interstate 85 in between Gaffney and Blacksburg.

➨ **Directions:** The Peachoid is located in Gaffney on I-85 near the exit for State Highway 11. For more information, visit www.gaffney-sc.com/waterpeach.htm or call 864-839-6742.

SOUTH DAKOTA

Largest Bull's Head
Porter Sculpture Park, SD

With its horns poking the sky of Interstate 90, the giant iron bull's head watches freeway drivers like a talisman. Wayne Porter made the behemoth. He calls it "The Bull's Head."

"I call my dog the dog. I call my black cat the black cat," says Porter.

But don't let the simplicity of his names fool you. A lot of thought went into the bull's head and the 50 other sculptures on the farmland west of Sioux Falls. The 25-ton bull's head took three years to build. It is made of railroad tie plates.

"The eyes are actually copies of Michelangelo's David," Porter says.

Inside are fake snakes, spiders, bats, and even a swing that Porter climbs up to.

Other sculptures in the park represent politicians (buzzards) and Porter's thoughts on life. He has a degree in political science so politics figures large, but there are also dragons and fish. He started out building with scrap metal and recycled farm materials. One dragon here is made of hot water tanks with eyes of bicycle reflectors. He'll tell you about the ideas behind the work, which he says usually teaches him a lot because of the interaction with other people.

Author photo

"Other people surf the net. I get tours. I run into more information that way," he says. He rents the 10 acres from a farmer.

➤ **Directions:** From I-90 take exit 374/Montrose. Head south for a half mile until you see a sign marking the entrance to the park. You'll travel one mile on a dirt road before you reach a small parking lot and shack where Porter might be waiting to give a tour. Admission is $4 per adult and children are free. The garden is open from 8

A.M. to 6 P.M. daily from Memorial Day to Labor Day. For more information, visit www.portersculpturepark.com.

Largest Pheasant
Huron, SD

Author photo

This giant bird was built in 1959, and after seeing the pheasant family in North Dakota, we're not sure he's the biggest. But both are worth seeing, and when you drive around the Dakotas enough, you start seeing these guys along the side of the street.

This guy was built to honor the pheasant population in the area. According to the state, the South Dakota Pheasant is 40 feet tall, a big bird in his own right. Stairways are set up on either side of him for good photo ops.

➤ **Directions:** Pheasant Phriend is located on Highway 14 about a half-mile east of Highway 37. He's next to a nice park, on the south side of the street, by the Dakota Inn. For more information, visit www.huronsd.com/chamber/ or call 605-352-0000.

TENNESSEE

Biggest Hot Dog, Fries, Burger and Soft Drink
Kingsport, TN

Who cares about King Kong size wieners when you can get a hot dog for $1.44? We've lived in areas that have their own local burger chains. (We wish we could have the Northwest's own Burgerville in here, but it doesn't have anything giant outside except Walla Walla onion ring signs, which we don't think anyone would travel to see.) But when we see an interesting burger chain out on the road, we know we're in for a treat. The first Pal's

Sudden Service opened in Kingsport in 1956. It served Sauceburgers and Frenchie Fries. After a second store was opened, a giant man holding a burger was placed on the roof to advertise the wares. The idea for giant food, such as burgers, fries, hot dog, and soft drink, came in the mid-80s. In 1985, two of the giant food stores opened in Kingsport.

➤ **Directions:** Pal's stores are located all over northeast Tennessee including Kingsport, Bristol, Johnson City, and other places. Giant food at many spots! For more information, visit www.palsweb.com.

Biggest Basketball
Knoxville, TN

Lodged into the north end of the Women's Basketball Hall of Fame is a big orange sphere. It'd be hard for even King Kong to play with it, even though its details are identical to a regulation ball. The basketball is made of steel and fiberglass and has more than 96,000 "nubs" just like on a real basketball. The ball weighs 20,000 pounds. Inside the hall, you can find 32,000 square feet of history, trophies, uniforms, videos of the top coaches, and even a figure of Senda Berenson, considered the "mother of women's basketball."

➤ **Directions:** The Women's Basketball Hall of Fame is located at 700 Hall of Fame Drive in Knoxville. From Interstate 40, take exit 388A/ James White Parkway. Turn left on Summit Hill Drive. Turn right on Hall of Fame Drive. Turn left on Hill Avenue. Admission is $7.95 for adults and $5.95 for children ages six to 15. The museum is open year round with longer hours during the summer. For more information, visit www.wbhof.com or call 865-633-9000.

Longest Live and Continually Running Radio Program
Nashville, TN

Back in the 1930s, people used to gather around their radios to hear the broadcast of country music from the Grand Ole Opry. Every Friday and Saturday night since 1925, a show has been broadcast from Nashville's WSM radio station. The Opry folks say that the first song broadcast was "Tennessee Waggoner" played on the fiddle by Uncle Jimmy Thompson.

Today you can listen to the show online. The Grand Ole Opry is the longest continuously running live radio program in the United States. NBC Radio started broadcasting the Grand Ole Opry in 1939.

➤ **Directions:** The Opry is located at 2802 Opryland Drive. From Interstate 24, take Route 155 east toward Opryland. Take exit 12, West McGavock Pike, toward Opryland. Turn right at McGavock Pike and left on Opryland. The Opry has regular live performances. The Grand Ole Opry Museum is open from 10 A.M. to 5 P.M. Monday through Thursday, from 10 A.M. to 8 P.M. on Friday, and from 10 A.M. to 10 P.M. on Saturday. Sunday hours are 11 A.M. to 4 P.M. For more information, visit www.opry.com or call 615-871-OPRY.

TEXAS

Largest Pair of Cowboy Boots
El Paso, TX

It took thousands of dollars in materials to make the largest cowboy boots—shoes not easy to fill. Made in 1999, the boots are five tall and nearly four feet long. It took a shopful of craftsmen two months to make them at Rocketbuster Boots. The style is called "Cool Arrows"; the green and brown boots are decorated with Native American profiles. Human-sized, one-of-a-kind boots are also made here by hand. There are stitched up boots with images of Christmas trees on them, boots with hula girls, and boots with the Olympic rings. Plenty of Texas styles have been made as well, including boots with oil wells and boots with Dallas Cowboy football players embroidered on the sides. The shop makes 500 pairs every year with a staff of six people. You can watch people working on them. The regular-folk sized boots are cheaper than the giant size, starting around $650 and heading up into the thousands. Famous customers, who include Arnold Schwarzenegger and Oprah Winfrey, can afford it.

➤ **Directions:** Rocketbuster Boots is located at 115 S. Anthony Street, two blocks from the convention center in the historic Union Plaza District of downtown El Paso. From Interstate 10, take the "downtown" exit which leads to Missouri Avenue. Turn left on Sante Fe Street, right on San Antonio Avenue, and then right on Anthony Street. Store hours are 10 A.M. to 5 P.M. Monday through Friday. Tours and fittings are given by appointment. For more information, visit www.rocketbuster.com or call 915-541-1300.

Largest Honkey Tonk Club
Fort Worth, TX

The first question, when faced with visiting the world's largest honky tonk is of course: what is a honky tonk? It is Billy Bob's. And according to Billy Bob's history, the building dates back to 1910. It was an open-air barn used for housing cattle during the Fort Worth Stock Show. In the 1930s, the city enclosed the building, creating a structure with stalls for more than 1,000 animals and an auction ring which was eventually transformed into Billy Bob's Bull Riding arena. But the building had other uses, too. During World War II, the space was used to build airplanes. In the 1950s, it was used as a department store that was so large, stock boys wore roller skates to get around more quickly.

In 1981, it opened as Billy Bob's Texas, with the Gatlin Brothers, Waylon Jennings, and Willie Nelson performing in the first week. BBT has even been in the *Dallas* television series. But it's not all about country. BB King and the Go-Go's have played there. The club does not have a mechanical bull, but there is real bull riding with live animals and real pro and semi-pro athletes sitting on top of them (all must have a valid rider's card to be permitted to ride.) Bull riding happens every Friday and Saturday night for a $2.50 charge. Dance lessons are also given. Billy Bob's Texas is 127,000 square feet, has 32 bars, and can hold more than 6,000 people at one time.

➼ **Directions:** Billy Bob's Texas is located at 2520 Rodeo Plaza. From Interstate 35, take exit 54B which is Northeast 28th Street. Head west toward Main Street and then turn left. Turn left on Stockyards Boulevard and watch for the club on the right. There is a cover charge which varies depending on what time you arrive. The charge starts at $1 if you come during the daytime, hits $2.50 on Friday and Saturdays, which covers the bull riding fee. It can be $6.50 and higher depending on the entertainment. For more information, visit www.billybobstexas.com or call 817-624-7117.

Biggest Fire Hydrant
Beaumont, TX

Somewhere in between the kindness of a fireman's Dalmatian and the influence of Walt Disney is a giant black–and–white spotted fire hydrant in Beaumont, Texas. According to the city, the hydrant was constructed at Disneyland in California as a promotion for the re-release of the *101 Dalmatians* video. Disney donated it to the city in 1999. In fact, according to the Beaumont Convention and Visitors Bureau, the spots on this hydrant are copyrighted by Disney and can not be reproduced. (So if you're dog has a similar appearance, you better take him to the vet.) This hydrant is capable of pumping 1,500 gallons of water through a sprinkler device on the top of the hydrant. The hydrant weighs 4,500 pounds and is 24 feet tall.

Directions: The big hydrant is located at the Fire Museum of Texas at 400 Walnut Street in Beaumont, which is 84 miles east of Houston. From Interstate 10, take the downtown exit, turn left at Calder and left at Mulberry. The museum is on the corner of Mulberry and Walnut. The museum is free and open 8 A.M. to 4:30 P.M. Monday through Friday. For more information, visit www.firemuseumoftexas.org or call 409-880-3927.

Longest Footbridge
Rusk, TX

This 546 foot bridge was originally built in 1861 just off the courthouse square to help people get around easier during the rainy season. The bridge was built before streets connected areas of town, so that townspeople could walk to the downtown business district when the creek flooded.

"When the floods came, that was the only way for people on that side of town to get into town," said Virginia Penney at the local chamber of commerce.

While it is long, it is not very high off the ground, so no fear of heights here. The version that exists today is not the original; the bridge was rebuilt in 1889 and restored in 1969.

Directions: Rusk is roughly 110 miles southeast of Dallas. From U.S. Highway 84, head into town and turn south on 5th Street. You should see the bridge after two blocks. For more information, visit www.rusktexas.com or call 903-683-4242.

UTAH

Largest Man Made Excavation
Bingham Canyon Mine, UT

You don't have to travel far to see this mine, if you're in Utah. You can see the behemoth from Interstate 15 as you drive around Salt Lake City. It looks like the mountain has melted or like someone tried and failed to make the world's largest Bundt cake. It is hard to comprehend the scope of this mine until you are up close and looking down into the depths of the pit. The mine is more than three-quarters of a mile deep and covers 1,900 acres. The Sears Tower (see Illinois superlatives) would only reach halfway up the mine.

It is said that the Bingham Mine is one of two man made creations visible from outer space. The other is the Great Wall of China. The mine dates back to 1863, when people from all over the world came to dig for precious metals. Miners have been surface mining this mountain since 1906 and are still pulling copper from the hills.

Today the place is run by Kennecott Utah Copper Corporation. According to the company's history, when Daniel Jackling started mining ore, which contained only two percent copper, he was laughed at by miners who believed the company could never make a profit. More than 100 years later, more than six billion tons of material has been excavated from here. The company has clearly figured out how to make money by mining low grade ore. According to the Visitor's Center, since 1906, more than 15 million tons of copper have been mined—enough copper wiring for every home and apartment in Mexico, Canada, and the United States.

The Visitor Center shows models of the pit and how it has grown over the years (and its projected growth over the next ten years). There's a movie that shows a blast and how open pit mining, or mining from the surface, is done. Crushed ore travels via conveyor belts to a processing center. A mill grinds it to powder and the tailings travel to Magma, a town nearby. The Center also has displays and history. Outside, the place is so big, there's even a traffic controller on staff to monitor all the activity of trucks and workers. Visitors are limited to the visitor center area.

Directions: The entrance fee is $4 per car. The Visitor Center is accessible from Highway 111. From I-15, take Highway 48/New Bingham Highway to 111. The Visitor Center entrance is four miles from the 48/111 juncture. From the entrance, you'll travel four miles up a well-paved road to the visitor center, which overlooks the giant pit. The Visitor Center is open seven days a week from 8 A.M. to 8 P.M. from April 1 to Oct. 31, weather permitting. For more information, visit www.kennecott.com or call 801-252-3234.

Largest Natural Bridge
Glen Canyon National Recreation Area, UT

According to the National Park Service, the bridge is 290 feet tall and spans 275 feet across the river bed. The top is 42 feet thick and 33 feet wide.

Natural bridges differ from arches because they have been formed by water breaking through rock. Like most of the natural features that we travel to see, the earth's processes that caused this arch were millions of years in the making. The rock that makes up Rainbow Bridge is sandstone. The bridge was formed by an ancient tributary of the Colorado River. The water eroded away weaker parts of the rock and left the stronger parts—the bridge—behind.

The bridge has been considered sacred by Native Americans for centuries. Theodore Roosevelt wrote about a 1913 trip, where all his traveling companions passed under the bridge except one: a Navajo man whose "creed bade him never pass under an arch." President William Howard Taft created Rainbow Bridge National Monument in 1910 to preserve the site. Visitors have flooded the site since the damming of the Colorado River and the creation of Lake Powell, which made getting to Rainbow Bridge easier. In 1974, Navajo tribal members who lived nearby filed suit in U.S. District Court against the Secretary of the Interior, hoping to preserve Navajo religious sites that were being buried under water. The courts said that water storage was more important and the Navajo lost the suit. In 1980, the Tenth District Court of Appeals ruled that closing Rainbow Bridge for Navajo religious ceremonies would violate the constitutional rights of other citizens.

The Park Service has tried to balance the needs of park visitors with the tribes affiliated with Rainbow Bridge. The Park Service asks that people who visit the bridge do so in a respectful manner. Since 1995, the Park Service has asked visitors to refrain from approaching or walking directly under Rainbow Bridge.

➤ **Directions:** Rainbow Bridge is accessible by boat or by a 13 mile hike, which requires a permit from the Navajo Nation. For more information, visit www.nps.gov/rabr/ or call 928-608-6200.

Biggest Disco Ball
Salt Lake City, UT

Derek Dyer wanted to break a record since he was a kid. As an artist who created large projections on buildings, a giant disco ball seemed like the perfect record to set. He collected materials and raised money for a year. Then he spent another year building the giant globe, which has a 10-foot diameter. It is modeled after an exact disco ball. The mirrors are five inch squares. He finished it just in time for New Year's Eve 2002 and unveiled it at Salt Lake City's "First Night" celebration. He calls it the Diversity Ball.

Credit: Derek Dyer

"I built it as a way to promote diversity," said Dyer. "We are all mirrors of one another. A disco ball gives you thousands of different perspectives." Now the dance inspiration is in demand and sometimes leaves its perch in the Mainly Art Gallery inside Crossroads Mall in Salt Lake City.

➡ **Directions:** The biggest disco ball was most recently displayed in downtown Salt Lake City in Crossroads Mall but is expected to move in 2005. Check www.derekdyer.com to find its current location.

VERMONT

Longest Covered Bridge
Windsor, VT

The Cornish-Windsor Bridge is the longest wooden bridge in the United States and the longest two-span covered bridge in the world. The one you see here is the fourth built on this site since the first one in 1866, which cost $9,000. The structure is 460 feet long and spans the Connecticut

River, which separates New Hampshire and Vermont. On the Vermont side is Windsor and on the New Hampshire side, Cornish Mills.

The bridge was first built by Bela Fletcher and James F. Tasker in the 1800s using a lattice truss patented by architect Ithiel Town. The bridge was built as a toll bridge by a private corporation but was purchased by New Hampshire in 1936 and made toll free in 1943. You can drive across it but there is no designated area for pedestrians. It's easy to get a photo from the New Hampshire side, as there's a scenic view turn-off just south of the bridge next to the sign.

➤ **Directions:** From Interstate 91 in Vermont, take exit 8. Get on 5 north toward Windsor. Turn right at Highway 44, also aptly called Bridge Street, and almost immediately you will cross the bridge.

Smallest State Capital
Montpelier, VT

With less than 10,000 people, Montpelier calls itself "intimate". The city was originally chartered in 1781. The population hasn't changed very much in the last century. In 1900, 6,266 people lived in Montpelier. Recent counts put the number of occupants at 8,400. When the state government was looking for a home, they chose Montpelier because of its central location and because local residents supplied land and money. The city had a couple statehouses before the current one was erected in 1859. Along with the statehouse's gold leaf dome, visitors can check out the Vermont Historical Society Museum, art galleries, parks, and take historic walking tours through the architecture.

➤ **Directions:** The city is located in a valley along the Winooski River in Central Vermont. For more information, visit www.montpelier-vt.org/ or call 800-837-6668.

Largest Syrup Can
St. Johnsbury, VT

Maple syrup farms and products dot the landscape in Vermont. Dakin Farm in Ferrisburgh, Vermont, has a giant syrup bottle. Maple Grove Farms in Vermont caught our eye with a roadside can. The tree lovers here say they are the largest packer of Pure Maple Syrup in the country and the largest maker of maple candies in the world. They've been tapping trees since 1915. You can tour the factory, buy maple products in the gift store,

Author photo

and learn more about syrup. Did you know that it takes up to 40 gallons of sap to produce one gallon of pure natural maple syrup?

Directions: Maple Grove Farms is located in St. Johnsbury at 1052 Portland Street. From Interstate 93, take exit 1 to Route 2 West. The factory is 2–1/2 miles on the left. The can is outside the building. Tours are given from mid-May to late-December from 8 A.M. to 2 P.M. Monday through Friday, except major holidays. For more information, visit www.maplegrove.com or call 802-748-5141.

VIRGINIA

Oldest Cured Ham
Smithfield, VA

We've seen a lot of meat in our day, but nothing quite rivals the oldest Smithfield ham—a piece of swine that has been hanging around since 1902. Smithfield hams are a special, salty ham cured in Smithfield.

Diane Hayes, an administrator at the Isle of Wight County Museum, says the ham has a "storied" history. It was probably ordered through a catalog or telephone sale at the turn of the century. Sometime before it was delivered, the poor pork got lost in the mail and was returned to the plant. Someone hung it in the corner and forgot about it for 25 years. It seems that the method used to cure hams back then could keep them fresh for years. The ham originally weighed more than 18 pounds, but when it was found after a couple decades, it had lost about 65 percent of its weight. Still, after it was found, it became famous. After 1924, the plant owner, P.D. Gwaltney, Jr., kept the ham in a safe and would show it off to visitors. It was used in an advertising campaign for the company, demonstrating how well-preserved their hams were. He had the ham insured against fire and theft and then he took the ham around the country and showed it at food fairs. Gwaltney even made a collar for the ham so he could chain it to the table when it was on display. Today, it sits in a glass case in the museum. It is not refrigerated or air tight, but it remains intact.

"Occasionally we have to put more pepper on it," said Hayes. "If you really get up to it close, there's kind of a musty smell. I don't think anybody would want to eat it." But we do want to see it. The Isle of Wight museum offers several aspects of local history, but we're interested in the areas devoted to old foods. There is also a vintage peanut in the museum that is more than 100 years old. That, too, was owned by P.D. Gwaltney, Jr.

The museum has some history on the hams, as well as a video of an event in 2002 when the town constructed the world's largest ham biscuit. That's not still around, but you can get a very cool white, oval, European-country-designation-style bumper sticker that says simply, "HAM."

➡ **Directions:** The Isle of Wight County Museum is located at 103 Main Street. From Route 17, head south on Highway 258, into Smithfield. Turn right on Route 10 West Business to the intersections of Church and Main Streets. The hours are 10 A.M. to 4 P.M. Tuesday through Saturday, and 1 P.M. to 5 P.M. on Sunday. Admission is free. For more information, visit www.co.isle-of-wight.va.us/park_rec/museum.html or call 757-357-7459.

Largest Kugel
Richmond, VA

First off, a kugel is a floating ball sculpture. The Science Museum of Virginia's "Grand Kugel" is a 29-ton granite ball that floats on water in front of the museum. It's nine feet in diameter and was made from Bon Accord granite mined in South Africa. The base is Tarn granite from France. The black, shiny ball is a scale model of the earth, and it rotates on its own, but visitors can move it to change its direction. Stop by and move the earth! There's a smaller moon kugel here too, about 250 feet away from the earth. The museum asked Kusser Granitwerke of Germany to make the ball, but first the Germans turned the job down, saying their machinery couldn't handle a project so large. A year later they came back and said they could modify their equipment to make it work. Kugel is German for "ball." The base of the kugel is connected to a water pump. When the system is turned on, it pumps 33.81 pounds per square inch—less than the pressure of a household faucet but enough to raise the kugel about the base. The project cost more than $1 million.

Credit: Science Museum of Virginia

➤ **Directions:** The museum is located at 2500 W. Broad Street. For more information, visit www.smv.org or call 800-659-1727.

Largest Naval Complex
Norfolk, VA

The ships here are so large, it's hard to understand how they float, let alone sit upright. Naval Station Norfolk is home to 70 ships in the Atlantic fleet. You can take a 45 minute tour narrated by Navy personnel who'll tell you about the training center, aircraft carriers, amphibious assault vessels, and submarines. According to the Navy, the station occupies roughly 4,300 acres on the peninsula known as Sewell's Point. It's the world's largest naval station and also the biggest naval installation in the world, based on military population. Apart from dozens of ships on 13 piers, the station is home to more than 130 aircraft, including helicopters.

➤ **Directions:** Tours depart from the Naval Tour and Information Center located at 9079 Hampton Boulevard in Norfolk. From Interstate 564, take exit 276 toward the base. Turn left at Virginia Route 337. For more information, visit www.navstanorva.navy.mil/ or call 757-444-7955.

Largest Bridge-Tunnel Complex
Virginia Beach, VA

The Chesapeake Bay Bridge Tunnel is the world's largest bridge-tunnel complex. It is a 17.6 mile route across the Chesapeake Bay. The bridge travels over and under the open waters of the Atlantic Ocean as it moves into the Chesapeake Bay. The result is a route between southeastern Virginia and the Delmarva Peninsula. It opened in 1964 and has carried more than 80 million vehicles over and through the water. The "complex" is made up of 12 miles of low-level trestle, two one-mile tunnels, two bridges, two miles of causeway, and four manmade islands.

➤ **Directions:** For more information, visit www.cbbt.com.

Credit: Chesapeake Bay Bridge-Tunnel

WASHINGTON

Largest Frying Pan
Long Beach, WA

Fry me a clam! Long Beach, which also has signs stating it's the world's longest beach (which we have not tried to confirm) is home to a gigantic black frying pan in the middle of this small coastal town. In the past, townspeople used to carry around this frying pan in the back of a pickup truck. In the 1940s, ladies in bikinis, along with the giant frying pan, traveled around to promote the annual Clam Festival held here. Even then, it was known as the "world's largest frying pan". There is a kiosk of photos just down the street between 3rd and 5th Streets, where you can see photos of chefs using the pan to make the "world's largest chicken fritter."

A giant clam sits next to the pan, but it doesn't really look like a clam. It looks like a big wooden bottle. It squirts water, but was broken when we visited. Across the street is a worthy stop. Although not officially a superlative, Marsh's Free Museum, here since 1921, surely has the most crazy old games, knickknacks, and oddities for sale in one place. There's old baseball pinball, a palm reader, the love tester, and other 5 and 10 cent games. You can dump a mini scooper into a pile of shells for five cents!

➤ **Directions:** The frying pan is located on the corner of 5th Street and Pacific Avenue on the main strip of shops in Long Beach.

Longest Hiking Trail
Pacific Crest Trail

The mother of all hiking trails runs up and down the peaks of the Sierra Nevada to Oregon's Mt. Hood and the Washington Cascades. The Pacific Crest Trail covers 2,650 miles between the U.S. borders of Canada and Mexico. (The famous Appalachian Trail, which runs from Georgia to Maine, is 2,174 miles.)

The Pacific Crest Trail climbs past Lake Tahoe and Crater Lake; crosses the Columbia River between Washington and Oregon, and skims Mt. Rainier National Park in Washington. The trail has the highest elevation changes of any of the country's National Scenic Trails. It hits dry deserts, wet forests, and even freeways. You don't have to hike the whole thing, but some people do. According to the Pacific Crest Trail Association, every year, about 300 people attempt to become "thru hikers," and walk all the way from one border to the other. Less than 200 usually finish the hike.

Author photo

The trip takes five to six months if you're hiking an average of 20 miles a day. "Thru hikers" designate check points along the route where they or their friends have mailed supplies. They also get off the trail briefly in cities for food, showers, phone calls, and a cheeseburger. Many more people test out the trail on shorter hikes; the route was first explored in the 1930s by men from the YMCA. Two men, Clinton Clarke and Warren Rogers, began lobbying the federal government for border to border access. For many years, the trail was a patchwork of disconnected segments that didn't hook up.

In 1993, the trail was officially dedicated as a completed trail. The trail is designated as "non-mechanized," meaning it is open to foot and horse travel only. Bicycles and motorized vehicles aren't allowed.

➡ **Directions:** There are many access points to the Pacific Crest Trail in Washington, Oregon, and California. For more information, visit www.pcta.org or call 916-349-2109.

Biggest Building (by volume)
Everett, WA

When you build airplanes, you need a big space. The Boeing Company has the largest building by volume in the world—472,000,000 cubic feet. After the company decided to build 747s, it needed a building big enough to do so. The Everett factory, 30 miles north of Seattle, was completed in 1968. You can tour the building and check out the production of 747s, 767s, and 777s.

➡ **Directions:** From Interstate 5, take exit 189 to State Highway 526. Drive 3 and one half miles and follow signs to the tour center. Tours are generally given Monday through Friday with periodic closures usually near holiday dates. Call ahead. Tickets are $5 for adults and $3 for children under 15. For more information, visit www.boeing.com/companyoffices/aboutus/tours/ or call 800-464-1476.

Largest Concrete Dam
Grand Coulee, WA

The Grand Coulee Dam holds back the Columbia River from running wild through Oregon and Washington. Work began on the dam in 1933. Today it provides electricity to the Northwest, as well as flood control and irrigation to neighboring farmlands. The dam cost $56 million to construct. It's 550 feet high and is made up of more than 11 million cubic yards of concrete. According to the U.S. Bureau of Reclamation, Grand Coulee's power production facilities are the largest in North America. Its irrigation potential can supply water to more than one million acres of land. It is the largest concrete structure ever built. All this, and a laser light show! Laser light shows are held nightly at the dam in the summer months.

➨ **Directions:** Grand Coulee Dam is located roughly 90 miles west of Spokane. You can reach it from State Highways 155 and 174. The U.S. Bureau of Reclamation Visitor Arrival Center is located on Highway 155 just north of the dam. For more information, visit www.usbr.gov/pn/grandcoulee or call 509-633-1360.

Biggest Red Wagon
Spokane, WA

Sculptures are usually best when you can slide down them. Artist Ken Spiering made a giant red wagon for Spokane that doubles as a slide. (You slide down the arm of the wagon.) The wagon weighs 26 tons, is 12 feet tall, 12 feet wide, and 27 feet long. It was made with reinforced concrete and can hold as many as 300 people.

➨ **Directions:** Riverfront Park is located in downtown Spokane. The park is a city-operated and has 100 acres filled with everything from regular old park barbecues to an IMAX theater and rides. The wagon is on the south side of the park. From Interstate 90, take the Division Street exit. Head north and turn left/west on Spokane Falls Boulevard. The wagon is in the park near Stevens and Spokane Falls Boulevard. For more information, visit www.spokaneriverfrontpark.com or call 800-336-PARK.

WEST VIRGINA

Largest Teapot
Chester, WV

According to the Hancock County Convention and Visitor's Bureau, the teapot was once a giant barrel used for a Hire's Root Beer advertising campaign. In 1938, William "Babe" Devon bought the barrel and had it converted into a teapot. A spout, handle, and tin were added to seal the deal. Local kids ran a souvenir store inside the teapot.

During its long history, the teapot store sold lawn and garden items and food. It was owned by several people, painted different colors, and shut down several times. In the 1980s, a telephone company bought the land where the teapot was located and donated the teapot to the city of Chester. The teapot wasn't fully restored until the 1990s, when the concession stand doors and windows were sealed shut. The teapot was moved to its present location, where it remains today.

➤ **Directions:** The teapot sits at the junction of State Route 2 and U.S. Highway 30. For more information, visit www.hancockcvb.com or call 304-387-2820.

WISCONSIN

Largest Six-Pack
LaCrosse, WI

The brewery in downtown LaCrosse has quite a history. Take a tour and you will appreciate what the City Brewery has gone through to stay open—several owners, hard times, and even the loss of one of its famous brand names, "Old Style". The World's Largest Six Pack used to be Old Style, but due to corporate maneuvering, the name is no longer owned by the City Brewery. But no tears! You can still get a good photo and some free beer (after the tour) in downtown LaCrosse.

The World's Largest Six Pack is an impressive sight. It is indeed full of beer, which is waiting to be bottled and canned on site. They say there is so much beer in one of the cans, you'd have to drink one beer every hour from the moment you're born until you're 125 years old to finish one. (Or something like that. It's a lot of beer—enough for more than 7 million cans

Author photo

altogether.) Even so, the motto of the brewery is still, "We didn't aim to make the most beer, only the best." On the tour you can hear the legends of the founder, John Gund, who started brewing beer in 1856.

➤ **Directions:** The World's Largest Six Pack is located at the City Brewery in downtown LaCrosse at 1111 S. Third Street. From I-90, head south on Highway 53. The hours vary by season. From June through Oct. 8, tours are held Monday through Saturday hourly from noon to 3 P.M. For more information, visit www.citybrewery.com or call 608-785-4820.

Biggest Talking Cow
Neillsville, WI

Chatty Belle lives in the parking lot of the WCCN radio station just outside of Neillsville. Like a couple of other superlatives in the book, she was made for the 1964 World's Fair in New York and came back home to roost after the fair ended. You have to pay 25 cents to hear her talk, but she will tell you a bit of her story. She is too distraught to mention that she had a little bovine friend by her side for some years. (You can see the second cow in postcards inside the gift/cheese shop. Good string cheese!) The little cow was vandalized years back and now Chatty stands alone. She's 16 feet high and 20 feet long—seven times larger than your average Holstein. On the site, there is also a replica of the "Golden Giant"—the world's largest cheese. The cheese, when it was real, was also at the World's Fair. Now it's just cardboard replacement stuck in a trailer.

According to the World's Fair Collector's Society, the building, called the Rotunda, was also at the fair and showcased Wisconsin's history, universities, and highways. The state was prepared to demolish the pavilion after the fair until a Wisconsin man offered to buy it for $5,000. Ivan Wilcox moved the Pavilion to his hometown of Boscobel, but once there, the town members were not interested in the idea of resurrecting it. Wilcox sold the building in 1966 to Central Wisconsin Broadcasting.

➡ **Directions:** Chatty Belle is located on Highway 10 just east of Neillsville, in the parking lot of the WCCN radio station. For more information, call 715-743-3333.

Largest Badger
Birnamwood, WI

Wisconsin is Badger Country, as any college football mascot lover knows. This guy is peeking up from the ground in front of a club, which is now a home to exotic dancers. He's really just a giant head and claws, but behind him is a giant fake tree trunk which might interest nature lovers.

➡ **Directions:** The badger is located just north of County Road ZZ on Highway 45, just outside Birnamwood.

Largest Muskie
Hayward, WI

Jumping out of the ground like evolution in motion, the leaping muskie is a "shrine to anglers" set up as part of the Freshwater Fishing Hall of Fame. His interior is a museum and his jaw an observation platform that can hold 20 people. The Largest Muskie is five stories of fiberglass fish. The museum has fishing memorabilia—old lures, antique rods, old motors, and 200 species of fish. Its goal is to present the artifacts of fresh water angling or fishing, as it is usually called. The landmark fish is protected by

Author photo

a design patent, so don't get any funny ideas about building one of your own. Jim Beam helped get the fish off the ground. In 1971, a special Jim Beam fishing decanter was issued with proceeds going to the Hall.

➤ **Directions:** The hall is located 70 miles south of Duluth in Hayward. From Highway 63, take a right at Highway 27. The giant fish is on Highway 27 on the left side. You can see the fish without entering, but you can't get up-close access unless the museum is open. Summer hours, from April 15 to Nov. 1, are 10 A.M. to 4 P.M. everyday. Admission is $6 for adults, $3.50 for children ages 10-17, and $2.50 from ages 2 to 9. For more information, visit www.freshwater-fishing.org or call 715-634-4440.

Author photo

WYOMING

Fewest People
Wyoming

Beautiful mountains. Wind swept plains. Rivers. Rodeos. Why don't more people live in Wyoming? It's the ninth largest state in the country, yet even more people live in Alaska than in Wyoming. According to the state's figures, Wyoming had just over 500,000 residents in 2003. (In 2003, roughly 640,000 people lived in Alaska.) Truly, you can enjoy wide open spaces in Wyoming.

Biggest Jackalope
Douglas, WY

Douglas calls itself the home of the Jackalope, a mythical creature that appears to be part jackrabbit and part antelope, we think—kind of like a 11-foot bunny with antlers. There's a large one in the middle of Douglas town square, but he's no prima donna. Over time, the local jackalope has seen hard times. In the 1960s, town merchants offered a $200 reward for information on the vandals who bent his horns so that they were facing the street. Leonard Lore created the hybrid from cement and steel for the town's Chamber of Commerce. But don't get any funny ideas about making one of your own; the jackalope is trademarked in the state of Wyoming by the Douglas Chamber of Commerce.

Credit: Douglas Area Chamber of Commerce

➡ **Directions:** From Interstate 25, take the Douglas exit toward the center of town. For more information, visit www.jackalope.org.

Oldest National Park
Yellowstone, WY

We have done a lot of traveling around this country, and Yellowstone never ceases to amaze. Clearly, superlatives are all over the National Park System . . . that is in part why we have it—to preserve the great national beauty of the country. It takes care of the world's biggest arch in Utah and the gigantic cave system in Kentucky. We've got amazing coastal parks and desert landscapes; the National Park System has all kind of landscapes to show us. But there is nothing like seeing geothermal energy at work in Yellowstone. Geysers propel water into the air. The earth bubbles in mud pots. This place is amazing. According to the Park Service, nowhere else in the world can you find so many geysers, hot springs, mud pots, and fumaroles. More than 75 percent of the world's geysers are right here in this park. Yellowstone has 10,000 hydrothermal features, the most famous being Old Faithful. It erupts on average every 92 minutes. A different geyser is taller; Steamboat is the world's tallest active geyser.

In the 1800s, people knew they had something special so they set it up as the first in the National Park System.

► **Directions:** Several highways enter Yellowstone, including Highways 20, 89, and 212. Some roads into Yellowstone close seasonally. The north entrance near Gardiner, Montana is the only park entrance open to wheeled vehicles all year. The entrance fee for vehicles is $20. Visitor Center hours vary seasonally. For more information, visit www.nps.gov/yell or call 307-344-7381.

ABOUT THE AUTHOR

Melissa Jones worked in a cubicle as a reporter for eight years in Idaho, Arizona, and Oregon, but she really prefers the open road. Her favorite car foods include strong, early morning coffee, afternoon beef jerky or cheese fingers, and when the passenger makes a sandwich with avocado on it. She grew up in Phoenix, Arizona and now lives with her husband in Portland, Oregon. Send feedback to melissa@superlativesusa.com.

Photograph of Author with Uncle Sam, the tallest American